"The book is an excellent and balanced history of separatism in Alberta. The very real factor of separatism in Alberta politics has been long overdue for examination."

- Cory Morgan
Former leader of the Alberta Independence Party

"Michael Wagner has performed a patriotic service by reminding Albertans (and Westerners) of what academics call a suppressed discourse. In this case it concerns the great fraud of national unity, which is code for ripping off the west in order to pay off Quebec, and the efforts of Albertans to stop picking up the tab."

- Barry Cooper, PhD, FRSC,
Professor of Political Science, University of Calgary

"This is a story well worth the telling, and well told indeed by a qualified and diligent researcher into the past half century of politics in Canada's other 'distinct society'. Apart from its being a tale of intrinsic interest to political junkies of all stripes, it does what Hobbes proclaims all worthwhile political history should do: secretly instruct the reader, conveying practical lessons of lasting importance. Moreover, in tracing out the reasons for the persistent waxings and wanings of separatist sentiment in Alberta, Wagner's account serves as an expose of how (mainly Liberal) Federal government policies have been designed to exploit the West, and Alberta in particular. This is a book that deserves to be read by every citizen concerned to understand this province's peculiar politics, and its place in the Canadian federation."

- Dr. Leon Craig,
Professor emeritus of
Political Science at the University of Alberta

ALBERTA
Separatism
Then and Now

By Michael Wagner

FR**E**DOM PRESS
CANADA INC.

ISBN 978-1-927684-32-0

FREEDOM PRESS
CANADA INC.

To Matthew Johnston

TABLE OF CONTENTS

GLOSSARY

AIP	Alberta Independence Party
APA	Alberta Political Alliance
ASP	Alberta Separatist Party
COR	Confederation of Regions Party
IAA	Independent Alberta Association
SPA	Separation Party of Alberta
WAP	Wildrose Alliance Party
WCC	Western Canada Concept
WIP	Western Independence Party
West-Fed	Western Canadian Federation
WNA	Western National Association

FOREWORD

L OOKING BACK A WHOLE QUARTER-CENTURY AND MORE, TO 1982, when I was young and easily convinced, I was a convinced western separatist. I voted for it with firm belief and would have taken up arms for it had duty called.

In 1982, I was living near Bowden, Alberta, and freelancing for my father's magazine, *Alberta Report*. Bowden lay just outside the rural constituency of Olds - Didsbury, so I was assigned to cover a provincial by-election there in February.

Not that there was much to cover. Of course provincial Tory candidate Stephen Stiles would go to the Legislature, and of course Lloyd Quantz would return to his cattle farm with the satisfaction of having carried the banner of rural Alberta's grand old party, the Social Credit. Ho hum. Six hundred words max, at 50 cents per.

On election morning, February 17th, I stopped in briefly at the Olds headquarters of Western Canada Concept (WCC) candidate Gordon Kesler. The whole top echelon of the new separatist party was on hand,

and many had been working the constituency for the past month. On the day of battle they evinced an unusual sense of expectation, and I saw a dangerous gleam in the eye of campaign manager Howard Thompson, from nearby Dickson.

It occurred to me then, for the first time, that they expected to win. They weren't just saying it. They actually felt it. They believed they had pulled off the election of the first western separatist MLA since the Northwest Rebellion of 1885.

I had met Kesler earlier that winter when he addressed a WCC rally in Grande Prairie. He spoke with a depth of emotion and quiet resolve which I felt just as strongly as he did, along with many, many others. It was a yearning to throw off the suffocating arrogance and socialist stupidity of eastern Canada, to build a real country with a real future, a country of which we could all be proud. It went far beyond hatred of Trudeau and French Power. It was impelled by a love of what was just, possible and good.

The Grande Prairie meeting was one of many short-notice events that winter. At any other time, it might have attracted a dozen cranky right-wingers, but that day it brought in hundreds of quietly furious, middle-of-the-road Albertans.

I liked Kesler personally. He was a Mormon from south of Lethbridge, a rodeo cowboy who ran a small business as an oil patch spy – someone hired by one oil company to watch and record the drilling progress of a competitor from off the lease. It's a perfectly reputable trade.

It was clear that the WCC message was moving through Alberta with a speed that could trigger the kind of political landslide for which our province is famous. February 17th in Olds-Didsbury would be the WCC's first test.

Hope springs eternally. After the polls closed that evening, I went first to Kesler's WCC headquarters, not Stiles', and from the first returns I knew I was in the right place. Kesler started out ahead in the Highway 2 corridor towns, and widened his lead as the count came in from further into the western hills. In the end he drew 4,015 votes, amounting to almost half of the popular vote. Neither of his competitors came close.

Kesler wasn't a drinker, but there was a euphoria in Olds that night I will never forget. Knowing my story had just gone from one page to six pages, I shot a cover picture of Kesler tipping his big white Stetson. Later, I hitched a ride with him and an oil patch friend of his (whose name I have unfortunately forgotten) to Edmonton.

Kesler spoke and I took notes as we rolled through the dark up Highway 2 in his light pickup, a stuffy little travelling bubble of joyful anticipation of the revolution to come. It was about 3 a.m. when we checked into the prestigious Hotel Macdonald. He and his friend, long used to living in hotels, pulled the mattress off the bed, found a cot, and we all bedded down in our clothes for a few hours of sleep. I then caught a cab to our Edmonton office and wrote a cover story. Such was my mood that it later won first prize for political coverage at the Western Magazine Awards in Vancouver.

But that was the high point. After that flash of happiness the iron laws of politics reasserted themselves. The movement was soon demolished by confusion of purpose, competing ambitions and organizational ineptitude.

I got a call from Kesler many years later. He was teaching high school on a Pima Indian reserve on the outskirts of Tucson, Arizona.

I'm glad my friend Michael Wagner has documented the rise and fall of that unusual movement, and analyzed the forces which drove it then, and might in some future circumstance drive it again. Perhaps next time will lead to a different outcome.

As for me, I have stopped thinking about separation. Over time, I realized there is more good to Confederation than we could see from under the heel of a National Energy Program imposed by the Ontario-Quebec Liberal Axis. And there is more to founding a country than getting mad. Federalism as we have inherited it is unsustainable; but it is not impossible.

The few who persist in separatist hopes (with exceptions like Doug Christie) remain generally oblivious to the preconditions necessary for its success. For many, it's a form of fantasy, which by daydreaming about they feel absolved of the hard and patient duties of government by consent of the governed.

The first and most obvious precondition for separation is a governing party in the Alberta Legislature able to do it. Only legislatures can separate from federations. The second essential is a list of fair demands of the federation that have been repeatedly submitted and repeatedly spurned. Only then, if ever, would most Albertans seriously consider separation. Mere "alienation" is not enough.

Still, despite its wild confusion and temper, the WCC did accomplish one thing. It established that Alberta, if provoked, might leave Canada. It helped advance the principle – now an established legal certainty – that any province, not just Quebec, has a constitutional right to peacefully secede. That, in turn, makes for a more cautious and reasoned federalism.

It's significant that never since Trudeau has Ottawa imposed on any province, or tried to impose, the kind of overt confiscation embodied by the National Energy Program.

This is not to say that "fiscal federalism" is fair to Alberta (or for that matter, Ontario). But its operation and effects are invisible, and most Albertans remain only vaguely aware they exist. The difference between the NEP and "fiscal federalism" is that the first was an invasion and the second a mere slow but deadly parasite.

Never since 1982 has Ottawa allowed a federal policy to prod into existence a provincial party which, on one year's notice and despite gross political ineptitude, can capture 12% of the Alberta vote.

In that paradoxical sense, the separatists were a force for national unity.

Link Byfield
Riviere Qui Barre, Alberta
February, 2009

PREFACE

THE VERY FIRST POLITICAL ORGANIZATION I EVER JOINED WAS WEST-Fed. I WAS only 15 years old. The second political organization I joined was the Western Canada Concept Party (WCC) of Alberta. By that time, I was 16 and the WCC had just won a by-election in Olds-Didsbury. During the provincial election campaign in the fall of 1982, I delivered promotional material for the local WCC candidate, Byron Chenger. At that point I was 17, not even old enough to vote. When the WCC failed to elect a single MLA, I was devastated.

A couple of years later, during the federal election campaign of 1984, I helped the local candidate of Elmer Knutson's Confederation of Regions Party (COR). This was the first election where I was old enough to vote, and of course, I voted for the COR candidate.

Early in 1987, one other fellow and I tried, unsuccessfully, to start an Alberta separatist student club at the University of Calgary, where we were undergraduates.

As I got older, other issues became more important to me. As well, Alberta's situation within Canada became less dire. I drifted away from the cause that had first inspired me to become involved in politics. But I still felt a special attachment to Alberta that did not extend to other parts of Canada.

Occasionally, I feel the same Alberta patriotism that made me into a fire-breathing, teenaged separatist. But intellectually, I now believe the case for Alberta separatism is much less certain. Things were different in the early 1980s. In particular, Pierre Trudeau and his crypto-socialist henchmen were waging economic war on Alberta. Due to the heavy concentration of voters in central Canada, federal elections offered no hope for Alberta's rescue. The only way to stop the pillaging was to get out of Canada. At the time, that was a compelling argument.

Things are different now, however. No subsequent federal government has attempted to raid Alberta, as Trudeau's had done. That's not to say we've had good governments at the federal level, but the situation has not been desperate from an Alberta provincial rights perspective. There's no pressing need for an immediate change in Alberta's political status.

Due to my interest and early involvement in separatist politics, I've often thought there should be a reasonably comprehensive book on Alberta separatism. Larry Pratt and Garth Stevenson's 1981 book *Western Separatism: The Myths, Realities & Dangers* contains some very helpful essays, but it was written too early to cover many important events. I hope my book will fill the gap and add new information and insights to an important part of Alberta's political history.

It's also important to give appropriate credit to a significant player in Alberta politics during the 1980s, *Alberta Report* magazine. This magazine was the media defender of Alberta during the Trudeau era, and it then made a vital contribution to the creation of the Reform Party of Canada. Alberta politics and Canadian politics were powerfully impacted by Ted Byfield's Edmonton-based magazine. *Alberta Report* may be gone but I hope a small portion of its spirit will live on in this book.

So am I an Alberta separatist? No. I don't consider myself to be a separatist, anymore. But I am a separatist sympathizer.

Intellectually, I'm not convinced that becoming independent is Alberta's best option. Continuing to remain within Canada is better for Alberta. However, that conclusion could change depending on future circumstances. Who knows if another Pierre Trudeau will appear, with a consequent attack upon Alberta? In this respect, it would be foolish to take the position that Alberta should never separate, come hell or high water.

Keep the options open. Alberta's situation within Canada is reasonably tolerable right now, but the future may contain some nasty surprises.

CHAPTER 1

INTRODUCTION

I N 1981, RICHARD CLEROUX, THEN-WINNIPEG BUREAU CHIEF OF the *Globe and Mail*, wisely wrote that "Western separatism is really Alberta separatism" (Cleroux 1981, 105). Separatist organizations have existed in the three other western provinces, but the real action has always been in Alberta. Alberta is the only western province where a separatist has been elected to the provincial legislature, and where separatist candidates have periodically made notable showings in general elections or by-elections, despite failing to be elected. Alberta is the most logical focus of any serious look at western separatism.

This book is the story of the Alberta separatist movement.

During the 1970s, a small group of Albertans, mostly Calgary oilmen, formed an organization called the Independent Alberta Association. They were disgruntled with the federal government's treatment of the oil industry and its apparent contempt for Alberta's exclusive jurisdiction over its natural resources. Therefore, they decided to explore the possibility of an independent Alberta.

Tensions mounted between Alberta and the central Canadian provinces over the increasing price of oil during the 1970s. Alberta was subsidizing central Canada by receiving much less than the world price for its oil. However, with the election of Joe Clark's Progressive Conservative (PC) minority government in 1979, it was hoped Alberta would get a better deal. This hope was dashed when Clark's government fell, and was replaced by a Liberal majority government under Pierre Trudeau in February 1980. Many Albertans believed that this election showed that Western Canada had virtually no influence on the national government, because elections were decided by Ontario and Quebec.

The result was the formation of a new pro-West organization called West-Fed, led by Edmonton businessman Elmer Knutson. Knutson denied being a separatist, but West-Fed was widely regarded to be a separatist organization. Also, Doug Christie, a BC lawyer, formed the WCC in an effort to promote Western separatism.

In October 1980, the Trudeau government introduced the National Energy Program (NEP). The NEP was widely viewed as an attempt by the federal government to seize control of Alberta's oil. Arguably, it was the most socialistic peacetime power-grab in Canadian history. The whole province erupted in anger, and the oil patch, in particular, was radicalized. Support for separatism soared, and a few prominent citizens even publicly declared support for western independence.

Both West-Fed and the WCC held large meetings across Alberta. The most famous was a WCC meeting at the Edmonton Jubilee Auditorium in November 1980. Doug Christie received standing ovations from an audience estimated at 2500, the largest separatist meeting ever held in Western Canada.

The WCC subsequently organized a provincial political party in Alberta, and it was put to the test in a by-election in a rural constituency north of Calgary, in February 1982. The Alberta WCC candidate, Gordon Kesler, won a convincing victory and support for the WCC took off.

However, the Alberta WCC became discredited by infighting and leadership squabbles. When Premier Peter Lougheed called an early general election for November 1982, the WCC did not win any seats, despite receiving almost 12% of the total provincial vote. At this point, it seemed that the Alberta separatist movement had received a fatal blow. The WCC had been discredited by constant infighting, weak leadership, and electoral defeat.

Pierre Trudeau resigned as prime minister, and in the federal election of September 1984, the PCs under Brian Mulroney won a majority government. Alberta had voted for the PCs on a massive scale, and it was believed the province would receive a better deal from the new federal government. Support for separation largely dissipated.

But the Mulroney Tories proved to be a big disappointment for westerners. Much of the PC caucus consisted of MPs from central Canada, including the Prime Minister himself. They were not particularly sensitive to Alberta's concerns. Once again, anger began to build in Alberta toward the federal government, especially after it awarded the CF-18 jet maintenance contract to a Montreal company, despite a western company having a better bid.

Support for separatism began to build steadily. The Alberta WCC was coming back to life. In a November 1987 by-election in central Alberta, Alberta WCC party leader Jack Ramsay came in second. The separatist WCC, which had been struggling since its 1982 general election defeat, had re-emerged as the Tories' main rival in some parts of Alberta.

After that encouraging by-election result, however, the Alberta WCC would never run another candidate for election. What happened? Why did a party that was making a comeback suddenly disappear? It disappeared when the Reform Party of Canada began to absorb voters who were interested in Alberta separatism.

Many who had been involved in Alberta separatist politics were not actually devoted to breaking up Canada. They simply wanted a fair deal for Alberta. When Alberta was getting ripped off by Pierre Trudeau, separatism seemed to be the best solution. Later, when the Mulroney government was blatantly favouring Quebec at the West's expense, separatism again became attractive.

However, by 1987, efforts were underway by prominent citizens, most notably Preston Manning, to build a non-separatist, western-based federal party which would represent the West's interests in Ottawa. The Reform Party of Canada did not suffer from the infighting and leadership squabbling that afflicted the WCC and other separatist groups. It was a credible organization which defended Alberta's interests within Canada, while avoiding the embarrassing public displays associated with other separatist groups. Further, separatist tendencies were contained within (and moderated by) a non-separatist organization.

The Reform Party had a profound impact on Canadian politics, but it was sacrificed in an effort to unite right-of-centre voters in Canada when it was folded into the Canadian Alliance, in 2000. Voters in eastern Canada, however, were largely uninterested in the Canadian Alliance in the November 2000 federal election. Resentment at the election results turned some Albertans toward separatism again. Without the Reform Party to articulate Alberta's concerns, the separatist movement began to organize meaningfully for the first time since the 1980s.

Stephen Harper became leader of the Canadian Alliance in 2002, and then led it into a merger with the PC Party in 2003, forming the Conservative Party of Canada. Harper had been a key Reform Party figure, so when he was elected prime minister in January 2006, Albertans knew he could be trusted to protect the province's interests. The potential growth of separatism in Alberta is being kept in check...for now.

But due to Canada's size and population distribution, it is very hard for the federal government to keep all regions happy. A federal government concerned about re-election will always be willing to appease the most populous provinces (Ontario and Quebec) at the expense of the others.

Stephen Harper is not immune to this reality, so his ability to promote reforms favoured by Alberta is extremely limited. If, at some later date, he is seen as having "sold out," separatism will surely grow. But the real potential for separatist growth will come after he leaves. The next prime minister is very unlikely to be as sympathetic to Alberta's concerns as is Stephen Harper.

In all likelihood, the federal government, at some future point, will upset many Albertans with some policy initiative or another. When that happens, there won't be a Reform Party to absorb and moderate the views of those who want to defend Alberta. Some other group will undoubtedly emerge to represent the concerned citizens of Alberta. And it's probable that separatists will be at the forefront of that effort. The demise of the Reform Party has removed the principal instrument for aggregating pro-Alberta sentiment into a moderate form. Thus the absence of the Reform Party leaves a void that will need to be filled. An invigorated separatist movement may be on Alberta's horizon.

REFERENCES

Cleroux, Richard. "Separatism in Quebec & Alberta" In *Western Separatism: The Myths, Realities and Dangers*, eds. Larry Pratt and Garth Stevenson. Edmonton: Hurtig Publishers Ltd., 1981

CHAPTER 2

THE EMERGENCE OF THE ALBERTA SEPARATIST MOVEMENT IN THE 1970s

ALBERTA POLITICS HAS LARGELY FOLLOWED A PATTERN OF ITS OWN, quite different from the rest of the country. Elections rarely toss out the government party. But when a party is tossed out, it's tossed out for good.

Not only that, but Alberta politics for many years was dominated by parties that had a negligible presence in other parts of the country – namely, the United Farmers of Alberta and then the Social Credit Party. In short, Alberta politics frequently differs from that of the other provinces.

Nevertheless, until the 1970s, the idea of Alberta becoming an independent nation was basically off the radar screen. Pierre Trudeau changed that. His policy of official bilingualism upset many westerners. And his subsequent policy of artificially suppressing the price of Alberta's oil led to anger across the province. Some oilmen formed the Independent Alberta Association (IAA) in 1974. The IAA then commissioned academic studies that laid the intellectual foundation supporting the case for Alberta separatism.

Although the IAA would fade away by the end of the decade, tension between Alberta and Ottawa continued to build toward the late 1970s. The Ontario Tory government of Bill Davis supported federal policy exploiting Alberta's energy resources for the benefit of central Canada. This exploitation was called "sharing." As Alberta's champion, Premier Peter Lougheed received considerable support from Albertans. But as the decade closed, the country was in the midst of a federal election campaign that would have very fateful consequences for Alberta.

MACLEAN'S MAGAZINE ON
WESTERN SEPARATISM, 1969

In July 1969, *Maclean's* magazine published a 5-page article on the emergence of separatism in western Canada. A growing number of people in the West were becoming fed up with how Canada was working. According to the article, each of the western provinces had its own concerns, but the entire region shared two particular beefs: the historical tariff system which discriminated against the West, and the new policy of official bilingualism implemented through the Official Languages Act.

Canada's first prime minister, John A. Macdonald, brought in the National Policy which established tariffs to protect industries centered in Ontario and Quebec. The effect was to benefit those provinces at the expense of the West. This had been a long-standing concern for people in the West. But the rise of nationalism in Quebec during the 1960s led the federal government to pay increasing attention to that province, and to introduce the policy of official bilingualism. Many people in the West began to think that Quebec could get whatever it wanted from the federal government, while the West's concerns were ignored.

To the degree that the Official Languages Act was an attempt to please Quebec, there's a sense that the perceived special treatment of Quebec sparked western separatism in its early form:

> It was the Official Languages Act more than anything else that led to the founding of the British Columbia Separatist Association in Vancouver by cabaret owner Bob Reeds, the Western Canada Separatist Movement in Edmonton by taxi driver Reg Wheatcroft, and the Dominion of Canada Party in Calgary by Mrs. Flo Frawley, president of a printing firm and a former Conservative Party official (Stewart 1969, 39).

The Dominion of Canada Party was not a separatist party but an English-language rights organization. Bob Reeds rented the Queen Elizabeth Theatre in Vancouver for a debate on western separatism, but less than 100 people attended the debate and Reeds lost a lot of money. The Edmonton-based separatist group was an even sadder story. As the *Maclean's* reporter relates, "The Western Canada Separatist Movement claims to have a substantial secret membership, but they are so secret I couldn't find any of them in two days of hard looking in Edmonton" (Stewart 1969, 39).

But he did find Dr. Hu Harries, former dean of commerce at the University of Alberta, and at that time a Liberal MP from Edmonton. Despite his Liberal Party affiliation, Harries was a solid westerner and was concerned about the West's place in Canada. He told the reporter:

> For years and years we'd cuss and swear at the east, but we had no place to go.
>
> Now we're a viable economic unit, and the rules have changed …I had my firm [an Edmonton-based company of economic consultants] prepare a budget on an independent west, and discovered that we'd have a hell of a surplus at today's tax rates …We want to maintain Confederation, and we don't mind accommodating Quebec, but when we have to pay for it, and at the same time we're excluded from the play, well, that's more than we can stand (Stewart 1969, 37).

Interestingly, Harries wasn't the only respectable citizen who had looked at the potential economic prospects of western independence in the late 1960s. "Two other studies, one financed by a retired Calgary oilman, the other by a group of federal and provincial political figures, came to the same conclusion as Harries' firm about the economic feasibility of an independent west" (Stewart 1969, 37).

Prime Minister Pierre Trudeau hadn't been around for very long, but he was already doing his part to generate support for separatism in western Canada. Before the oil crisis of 1973, the Alberta oil industry felt slighted because it was not permitted to sell oil to eastern Canada beyond southern Ontario. Alberta oil was shut out of Montreal because it was a little more expensive than foreign imported oil. Trudeau was asked about this issue when he visited Alberta:

> Prime Minister Trudeau ducked public discussion on the oil issue at a Calgary meeting, then told inquiring reporters, "I like to disappoint people sometimes." No campaign by his political foes could convince Albertans of Trudeau's indifference as effectively as that one glib statement (Stewart 1969, 37).

Prairie wheat farmers were also suffering at that time. Prices were down and unsold wheat stocks were at a record high. "Again, the Prime Minister found the perfect, infuriating remark when he asked farmers at a Winnipeg meeting, 'Why should I sell your wheat?'" (Stewart 1969, 37).

The rise of Quebec nationalism contributed to the rise of Pierre Trudeau to his position as prime minister. It was hoped that Trudeau could successfully accommodate Quebec within Canada, and thereby preserve national unity. But Quebec nationalism made many westerners uncomfortable, and Trudeau himself made many westerners angry. Although westerners had had grievances with Ottawa right from the earliest times of western settlement, it was those issues related to Quebec, bilingualism, and Pierre Trudeau that began to generate support for the concept of an independent western Canada.

There were certainly economic issues involved in western discontent, but there was more to it than that. The *Maclean's* article concluded as follows:

> "The main question is psychological," said Senator John Nichol. "The west has to be convinced that eastern Canada knows we're here, cares about us and is willing to do something for us."Without some sign soon of that knowledge, that care, that willingness, separatism could become a potent force across the Canadian west (Stewart 1969, 40).

That was prescient.

THE UNFINISHED REVOLT

The first book written on western separatism appears to have been *The Unfinished Revolt: Some Views on Western Independence,* a collection of essays published in 1971. The book's editors – John Barr and Owen Anderson – were significant because Barr was the executive assistant to Alberta's minister of education, and Anderson executive assistant to Alberta Premier Harry Strom. Both men were prominent figures in the final days of Alberta's Social Credit government.

University of Alberta political scientists Larry Pratt and Garth Stevenson described *The Unfinished Revolt* as "the first manifesto for separation" (Pratt and Stevenson 1981, 12). That assessment, however, is rather over-stated. For the most part, the essays comprising the book seem to favour decentralizing Canada, rather than western separation. Anderson states explicitly that "separation is presently out of the question" (Anderson 1971, 55). James Love takes a detailed look at economic issues and states that "The alternative to Confederation is balkanization" (Love 1971, 115). If balkanization were to occur, he says, "In all likelihood the standard of living would decrease or would increase only at the cost of joining the U.S. politically. From the West's point of view this is not the answer" (Love 1971, 115). So there's no apparent support for separation from him.

The final essay in the book, by Peter Boothroyd, is particularly anti-separatist. Boothroyd takes a very left-wing view and says that western separatism is "a conscious attempt by the local elite to gain more control for itself" (Boothroyd 1971, 135). Western grievances, as far as he

11

is concerned, are "the manufactured complaints of a colonial bourgeoisie complaining because it isn't getting its fair licks in at the people" (Boothroyd 1971, 142-143).

Only John Barr offers much real support for separation, but even his support is highly qualified. He outlines the situation this way:

> Conscientious Westerners must …try to make Canada work, but in a more just fashion. If, however, it becomes obvious that Canada is not a viable proposition politically, or if the present injustice deepens, I see no very persuasive moral argument for the West trying to integrate itself into a burning building. Therefore:
>
> 1. We must strive for a more justly constituted Canada;
>
> 2. If Canada loses her political viability, the West must strike out against the odds to try and build an independent State in this corner of North America (Barr 1971, 27-28).

That's basically a concise statement of what can be called a "soft" separatist position. First give Canada another chance. Then, only pursue separation after it's clear that Canada won't work, despite attempts at reform.

Barr had some other interesting things to say. According to him, in 1969, elements of the Canadian media "began to awaken" to the presence of some separatist sentiment in western Canada. They looked at separatist groups that existed at the time, "none of which are presently too impressive in either intellectual terms or in numbers" (Barr 1971, 14).

More interesting still, was Barr's assessment that westerners with the greatest degree of resentment were the Diefenbaker Tories. They were unhappy that their view of the country had been rejected. Barr states that:

> …close beneath the skin of every angry Westerner today you will find a one-time naïve Canadian nationalist who felt betrayed by the events of the 1950's and 1960's.

These Westerners (their number is Legion) supported John Diefenbaker for many reasons, one of the chief of which was his vision of nationalism. But the quiet revolution in Quebec and the growth of separatism confronted them with the fact that the "united Canada" they had always believed in had never really existed, save in their own heads. Thus, if it was true that Quebeckers felt no deep or abiding loyalty to the larger Canada, and Ontarians were largely using Confederation to cement their economic mastery over others, it was possible, just possible, that Westerners had been made the patsies of Confederation (Barr 1971, 22).

Many years later, there was a theory that the Reform Party of Canada in its early phase was basically the Diefenbaker wing of the federal Progressive Conservative Party. If so, in a faint sense, Barr's comments seem to foreshadow the support base for what would become the Reform Party.

INDEPENDENT ALBERTA ASSOCIATION

Early in 1974, Lloyd Gilmour, the publisher of an oil service industries magazine, *The Roughneck*, held two informal meetings at his home near Calgary. Together with some oilmen, he attempted to gauge support for western separatism. These meetings led to a larger meeting at the home of Mrs. Mildred Nelson of High River, whose husband was a well-respected rancher in the region.

That meeting was very successful, in the sense that support for separatism was strong. The IAA was thus formed, and prominent Calgary oilman John Rudolph (known affectionately as "Iron John" to some) was chosen as its president. Gilmour, Rudolph, and legendary Calgary lawyer Milt Harradence were credited as being the organization's founders.

As an oil company executive, Rudolph had been instrumental in the discovery of various oil fields in Alberta. During the 1960s, he had been the president of the Independent Petroleum Association of Canada (IPAC). In that capacity, he had traveled to Ottawa to represent his industry, only to encounter indifference from top bureaucrats. This made him angry.

13

In 1973, the Trudeau government imposed the export tax on oil which violated the principle of provincial resource ownership. Seeing that Quebec was benefiting from the fear that it may separate, Rudolph advocated that Alberta should do likewise. "Only by making the same threat, he says, can the West prevent itself from becoming a permanent hinterland, and only if it really means what it threatens will the threat be taken seriously" (*Saint John's Edmonton Report* 1974, 25).

By late 1974, the IAA had over 300 members in the prairie provinces, most of whom were in Calgary. The association's vice-president, Alderman Robert Matheson of Edmonton, was trying to set up a branch in his city.

Although the High River meeting had been successful, it had also exposed a weakness. As Rudolph himself put it, "We knew right away that we were in no position to lead the thing we had started. We lacked facts. We lacked plans. We lacked know-how. The first step was to get the facts" (*Saint John's Edmonton Report* 1974, 28).

Thus, the IAA decided to commission research reports that could provide the intellectual foundation for a successful Alberta separatist movement. The group was able to raise $40,000 for two economic studies about the viability of an independent Alberta. A separate study on the constitutional issues related to provincial independence was also undertaken.

The first economic study was conducted by Prof. Warren Blackman of the University of Calgary. It was released at a meeting in Calgary in November, 1974. About 120 people attended the meeting. Most of them were oil executives, but Tory MP Jack Horner was also present. There were a number of media people there too, including representatives of the *Financial Post* and the national network of the CBC (*Saint John's Edmonton Report* 1974, 25).

Blackman made it clear that Alberta was financially penalized for being part of Canada. His study compared Alberta as a province with a theoretically independent Alberta. He found that "the GDP of an independent Alberta rises faster than a Provincial Alberta, in fact, the increase is 2.4 times greater in the case of independence than the current Provincial status" (Blackman 1974, 87). Canada was a financial drain on Alberta: "As to the cost of Confederation from the opportunity cost point of view, we may state with reasonable certainty that it amounts to between 1 to 3 billion dollars per year (1.4 billion in 1974) in 1961 dollars…. This is a substantial sum, indeed" (Blackman 1974, 93).

The conclusion, therefore, was not hard to reach: "Could an 'independent Alberta' survive? The answer is, of course. Not only could the 'state' survive but it would prosper with a rising GDP of some 5% per year in this decade" (Blackman 1974, 92). So the first major study of the issue indicated that Alberta would benefit economically by separating from Canada.

The second economic study commissioned by the IAA appeared a year later, toward the end of 1975. This time Prof. Blackman was a co-author with economist Michael Hollinshead of Grant MacEwan Community College in Edmonton. This study demonstrated that it was the policies of the federal government that were the most responsible for Alberta getting a raw deal from Confederation, at least from an economic perspective. Hollinshead and Blackman suggested that "western alienation stems from a rigid, fossilized structure of policies which have originated and continue to emanate from Ottawa" (Hollinshead and Blackman 1975, 13). The authors concluded by stating, "we can say with reasonable certainty that the failure of the federal government to correct the many anomalies which are within its area of responsibility is the primary divisive force in confederation" (Hollinshead and Blackman 1975, 55).

By the time this study was written, there was already a perception in parts of Canada that Albertans were wealthy because of the province's petroleum resources. It was therefore assumed that Albertans should "share" their wealth. But the truth was that Albertans had basically the same average per capita personal income as people in other parts of Canada. So the federal government's confiscation of some oil revenue was not fair:

> With a personal income at practically the national average, federal expenditures have been consistently below the national average. Furthermore, in 1973-74, for the first time, taxes paid per capita exceeded the national average by 6.6%, largely the result of the oil

export tax. This is how resources are transferred from Alberta to the rest of Canada at the same time that per capita personal income remains at the national average. This is probably the most serious of the inequities (or inefficiencies) of the entire system of federal-provincial transfers. It means that Alberta's income is already "level" but Albertans continue to transfer their wealth out of the province by means of taxation of resource-based industries and low federal expenditures in the province (Hollinshead and Blackman 1975, 34-36).

It's not surprising, then, that they wrote, "Albertans, in a word, are not getting their money's worth out of confederation" (Hollinshead and Blackman 1975, 51).

Earlier in 1975, the IAA study of the constitutional issues involved in provincial independence was released. It was written by Patrick McDonald, an Edmonton lawyer and sessional instructor in constitutional law at the University of Alberta. McDonald was not an IAA member or a supporter of independence. His 84-page treatise covers the history of constitutional law, from Confederation to the mid-twentieth century. Basically, McDonald's argument was that the provinces (as colonies) existed prior to Confederation, and, in a sense, created the federal government. The provinces that were carved out of Rupert's Land and the North-Western Territory (Alberta, Saskatchewan and Manitoba) were granted equal status with the other provinces by the Queen's authority. Because the provinces existed prior to the federal government, and contributed to its coming into existence, each of them retains a right to pull out of Confederation.

Arguing on the basis of an important judicial decision, McDonald states that "the provinces are not subordinate to the Dominion, that they possess original legislative capacity, and that their governments are governments of Her Majesty" (McDonald 1975, 45). As a result of legislation passed by the British Parliament, Canada's Parliament was granted power to create new provinces out of Rupert's Land and the North-Western Territory, but these new provinces would be seen as being established by the British Parliament. "The provinces formed out of Rupert's Land and the Territory were constituted by federal legislation, but the essential attributes of provincial status were endowed by

16

the Queen in Parliament and not by the Parliament of the federation" (McDonald 1975, 47). The implication of this information is that "As provinces" Alberta and Saskatchewan "were not the creatures of the Dominion" (McDonald 1975, 47). This is important, because if Alberta and Saskatchewan were creatures of the federal government, they wouldn't have a right to secede from Canada.

As mentioned previously, McDonald argues that the provinces existed prior to the federal government, and did not lose their identity when they federated:

> The union provided for the continued exercise by each colony individually of certain of the powers previously possessed by each, and for the exercise by the colonies collectively of such of their powers as were considered to be of common concern to all. In the result, there was no welding into one of the constituent units, rather each remained independent and autonomous, and none was made subordinate to the central authority (McDonald 1975, 82).

The conclusion of this constitutional study was that "The federal system is now founded upon the sovereign will of each of the several provinces forming it, and unilateral secession of any province from the union is a matter of right, not of revolution" (McDonald 1975, 83).

The leadership of the IAA was smart. They realized they had little information with which to argue their case. Thus they commissioned these studies which provided an intellectual basis for arguing in favour of Alberta's independence. The IAA studies provided the intellectual foundation for the case for western separatism.

Studies in hand, the IAA transformed itself, in early 1977, into a provincial political party called the Western National Association (WNA). It was led by Edmonton feed lot operator Doug Low, who had been a proponent of direct political action within the IAA. Low had been a Social Crediter, and then a Tory activist, even a provincial PC riding association president. At the Calgary meeting where the WNA was inaugurated, Low asked the audience, "What is it to be a good Canadian?" and answered as follows:

> It is to: Produce grain and ship it through the Seaway. Produce oil and ship it through the pipeline. Store at our expense any item the central core area of Canada may need some time in the future. Buy all our goods from Canadian-protected central industries at inflated prices and pay full freight. Never attempt or consider to manufacture any of our raw products in the West, even for our own use. Pay full tax as set out by the Ottawa government and be loyal and patriotic citizens. Why should the breakfast cereal made from our own grain be processed in the East and shipped back to us? Why should the butter patties be packaged and processed in Montreal instead of somewhere in the West? The reason is simple. This is not the Canadian Way. Only the basic raw materials are to be produced here. All the processing, packaging and merchandising must be done in the protected industrial heartland where the federal voting control lies. Then when the processing is done, the colonies (the West) are to provide a captive market at any price for this imperialistic central core of Canada. It is easy to see why part of this industrial core area is called the Golden Horseshoe. Our sweat, toil and natural resources have made it that way (*Saint John's Edmonton Report* 1977a, 10).

At about the same time, the IAA released the findings of a survey conducted by Prof. Roger Gibbins, a political scientist at the University of Calgary. The survey was made for the Alberta Social Credit Party, but somehow the IAA had gotten hold of it. On the one hand, it indicated that there was very little support for Alberta's independence among the general population. But on the other hand, there was a very high degree of western alienation among Albertans:

> A deep and pervasive sense of alienation exists within the Alberta electorate. It is apparent that western alienation is more than a media creation, and more than the short-term consequence of energy disputes between

the provincial and federal governments. Rather, it exists as a broad public sentiment reflecting a sense of geographical and cultural isolation, political frustration, partisan bitterness and economic grievance. The extent of the phenomenon is such that minor changes in national policy beneficial to the West are unlikely to have a discernable impact in reducing alienation in Alberta (*Saint John's Edmonton Report* 1977b, 12).

A few weeks later a significant event occurred in Alberta politics: right-wing Tory MP and Diefenbaker loyalist, Jack Horner, left the federal PC Party to become a Liberal cabinet minister in Pierre Trudeau's government. Horner could not get along with PC leader (and notorious Red Tory) Joe Clark, and their conflict led to Horner's defection to the hated Liberals. Early, as this situation was developing, and Horner left the PCs, the Western National Party (as the WNA was then called) sent him a telegram inviting him to join.

Horner had, in fact, attended an important IAA meeting in 1974. Milt Harradence, one of the most prominent members of the IAA, was Horner's cousin. In 1976, Quebec had elected its first separatist government. As *Saint John's Edmonton Report* noted, "the total Canadian political picture would change if Quebec were to separate. Western separatism would gain instant credibility. With a man as well known as Mr. Horner as its leader, that credibility would be very much enhanced" (*Saint John's Edmonton Report* 1977c, 18). But, of course, Horner made the mistake of joining the Liberals, and therefore went down to a well-deserved defeat in the subsequent federal election of 1979.

The Alberta separatist movement was thus denied a potentially powerful leader in Jack Horner. Another significant candidate for leader of the movement was Milt Harradence. Harradence had been the leader of the Alberta PC Party before Peter Lougheed, but had become a separatist in the 1970s. He was a dedicated Diefenbaker loyalist, like Horner. In spite of that, Pierre Trudeau had Harradence appointed to the Court of Appeal of Alberta, in early 1979.

Harradence's biographer, C. D. Evans, posits the theory that the appointment was a deliberate ploy to prevent Harradence from emerging as a separatist leader. Evans states that in the Prime Minister's office

Harradence "was perceived – and actually feared – to be the natural leader of the Revolt of the Western Masses, the first president of an independent and totally loopy right-wing Alberta" (Evans 2001, 258). Apparently Harradence himself subsequently bought into this theory, for he later harangued Evans with "a two-hour diatribe about 'those bastards' plotting to appoint him so that he could not take Alberta out of Confederation" (Evans 2001, 260-261). It's just a theory, but it is plausible, considering that a person of Harradence's stature and abilities would have been the type of leader who could really have made a difference in the separatist movement.

Another leader with great potential, John Rudolph, resigned as IAA president in 1976. He then established a small oil company in Denver, Colorado. Frustrated with the Canadian government, he moved with his family to Denver in 1978 (*Saint John's Edmonton Report* 1978a, 24).

Rudolph's reputation as "Iron John," and as an opponent of the federal government, lived on after his departure for the United States. This became apparent in the following situation:

> In the early 1980s, following the imposition of the National Energy Program, former Alberta separatist leader John Rudolph occasionally flew to Calgary on business from his new home in Denver. On one such Western Airlines flight, the tall, craggy-faced Rudolph was recognized by a number of Calgary oilmen who were aboard the aircraft. A rumor raced through the plane that "Iron John" was coming home to renew the fight with Ottawa, which prompted a spontaneous standing ovation from dozens of passengers (Koch 2003, 54).

But alas, it was not to be.

THE ENERGY WAR OF THE 1970s

The most important backdrop to the rise of a substantial separatist movement in Alberta was the conflict over energy policy and oil pricing between the federal and provincial governments, from 1973 to 1981.

Before the early 1970s, there was some dissension in Alberta because it was difficult to sell oil due to widespread availability and low prices. There was basically an oil glut. Alberta received a little higher than world prices for oil during the 1960s, and into the 1970s, as a kind of subsidy for the oil industry. But the issue of Alberta's oil was not a major source of conflict between the provincial and federal governments.

Everything began to change in the fall of 1973. On September 3, 1973, the federal government of Pierre Trudeau imposed a federal oil export tax. This involved siphoning money out of Alberta, and to a lesser extent, Saskatchewan. Premier Lougheed at the time stated:

> This appears to be the most discriminatory action taken by a federal government against a particular province in the entire history of Confederation.... The natural resources of the provinces are owned by the provinces under the terms of Confederation. The action taken by Ottawa strikes at the very roots of Confederation (Wood 1985, 147).

And so the energy war began. But the real fun was just around the corner.

Oil had been cheap and plentiful throughout the 1960s and early 1970s. In the early 1970s it was valued at about a couple of dollars per barrel. In early October 1973, the Yom Kippur War erupted, and the Arab combatants called upon their fellow Muslim nations to cut off oil to the Western nations that supported Israel. Many of the largest oil producing countries were members of the Organization of Petroleum Exporting Countries, commonly known as OPEC. To make a long story short, "through ruthless negotiation in the four months between October 1973 and January 1974 the OPEC nations drove the international price from $2.75 per barrel of oil to over $11.50. The era of cheap energy was over" (*Alberta Report Supplement* 1979, 2).

The conflict between Alberta and the federal government over the energy issue was bitter. At one point toward the end of 1973, Alberta energy minister Don Getty had reached an agreement with federal energy minister Donald Macdonald. But Macdonald reneged on the agreement, and Getty publicly announced that Alberta couldn't trust the federal government to honour its agreements. Macdonald responded by publicly saying that Getty was "vicious" and "dripping with venom" (Wood 1985, 150).

During 1974, the federal government disallowed oil companies from deducting provincial royalties from their taxable income. Royalties were paid to the Alberta government because it owned the mineral rights in most of the province. Royalties were an expense the oil companies incurred, so it was only right that they should not be taxed on them. From an Alberta point of view, the new federal policy was outrageous. Later that year, Lougheed described federal oil policy as "probably the biggest ripoff of any province that's ever occurred in Confederation's history" (Wood 1985, 155).

Among the most significant federal policies was a freeze on the price of oil to protect consumers and industry. This was extremely unpopular in Alberta, because it meant the province was losing out on billions of dollars of revenue:

> The price freeze on oil, an extraordinary measure to take on a single commodity in peacetime, in effect was an enormous subsidy from Alberta to eastern Canada, unparalleled in Canadian history. The dollars saved for central Canadian industry were revenue Alberta would normally have been taking a percentage royalty from. The province was losing hundreds of millions of dollars, then billions (*Alberta Report Supplement* 1979, 3).

Under Premier Lougheed, Alberta fought back hard. Don Getty stated that "When we went to negotiations with the feds, I was authorized to bargain right up to (but not including) secession. Certainly if necessary we were willing to turn off the taps" (*Alberta Report Supplement* 1979, 3). And he reiterated this point: "We were determined to struggle almost to the point of secession for our right to set the price of our oil" (*Alberta Report Supplement* 1979, 4).

With the dramatic rise in the international price of oil, many people in eastern Canada wanted the federal government to hold down the price they would have to pay for energy, especially gasoline. This view held that:

> [T]he West should break time-honored traditions of Canadian regions supplying goods and commodities to each other at or often above the world prices. Now it was the duty of all Canadians to pull together in the national interest. Let the West supply everyone at a fraction of the going rate. The best known (if not the best) western response were the famous Calgary bumper stickers savagely urging "Let Those Eastern Bastards Freeze In The Dark." Decades of bitterness between west and east over oil and other matters were not about to be forgotten overnight (*Alberta Report Supplement* 1979, 2).

The stance of the Alberta government, and incidents like the afore-mentioned bumper stickers, contributed to a view in eastern Canada that Albertans were rich, greedy and selfish. Why weren't they willing to "share" with the rest of the country? But Premier Lougheed pointed out at the time, "the facts are that Ontario citizens still enjoy an average income much higher than Albertans" (Lougheed 1974, 62). Besides, Alberta was just asking to be treated in the same way as the other provinces. "If other regions of Canada are able to obtain fair market value for goods that can be easily replaced, Alberta is surely entitled to ask for the same in regard to the sale of resources which, once depleted, can never be renewed" (Lougheed 1974, 20).

Lougheed argued that Alberta's position was reasonable and would not be harmful to the country as a whole:

> There is a certain bitter irony for me, a convinced federalist all my life, in the complaints being leveled at my government, complaints that Alberta's energy policy is selfish and divisive, and that we don't care what happens to the rest of Canada. In fact, we care very much what happens to all of Canada; we just don't happen to equate all of Canada with Toronto, Montreal and Ottawa (Lougheed 1974, 20).

Lougheed had come to power in 1971 by ousting a Social Credit re-gime that had been in power since 1935. He called the subsequent provincial election for March 1975, asking voters to support him in his position on provincial rights and resources. This time he won 69 of 75 seats, basically wiping out the opposition. No one doubted Albertans' support of their premier during the energy war. As one source put it at the time, "Most Alberta people read Peter Lougheed's victory as a backup send-off for his anticipated give-the-East-hell follow-up campaign" (Ludwig 1975, 19-20). Ron Ghitter, a Tory MLA from Calgary was quoted as saying, "Peter will be the first provincial premier to stand up to the East – I mean really stand up – to Trudeau, to Ontario, to Quebec" (Ludwig 1975, 20).

As the price of oil increased, Alberta's income from royalties also increased. The Alberta government owned the mineral rights for most of the province, and it was therefore entitled to royalties on most of the oil and natural gas. But these resources would be depleted in a matter of years. So, in May 1976, Lougheed's government established the Heritage Savings Trust Fund, in order to save a certain percentage of resource revenue for future generations. It could also be used as an investment fund for diversifying the provincial economy. Apparently, Canadians outside Alberta were envious of the Heritage Fund.

A federal election was held in May 1979, and the Progressive Conservatives won a minority government under Joe Clark. There was hope that things would improve for Alberta under the Albertan Clark, but it wasn't that simple. Among other things, Clark had to contend with the Ontario PC government of Bill Davis, which was very antagonistic towards Alberta's demands for oil pricing and provincial control of resources.

In August 1979, Premier Davis released an energy policy proposal which said Ontario should help set oil pricing in Canada. "But for sheer effrontery, the proposal made for oil revenues was shocking to every Albertan who could understand its implications. The Davis document recommended closing Alberta's Heritage Fund and shifting new money from provincial royalties into the federal treasury" (Wood 1985, 159-160). It was categorically rejected by Alberta.

Alberta struggled through difficult negotiations with Joe Clark's government for an energy agreement. But once an agreement was finally reached, Clark's government fell in a vote of non-confidence in the House of Commons, in December 1979. An election was scheduled for February 1980, and a very fateful election it would be.

THE LIMITED APPEAL OF
SEPARATIST SENTIMENT IN THE 1970s

Despite the energy war, support for separatism in Alberta was not growing in any noticeable way. Certainly, many Albertans were angry at the federal government's policies limiting Alberta's ability to benefit from its resources, but this anger was not yet translating into separatist sympathies.

Professor Roger Gibbins, of the University of Calgary, conducted an opinion survey in the summer of 1974. It indicated that many Albertans believed the federal government was favouring Ontario and Quebec at the expense of western Canada. It also showed that Albertans who felt alienated from eastern Canada were very likely to support the Progressive Conservative Party. But support for separatism was low, and most of those surveyed hadn't even heard of western separatism (*St. John's Edmonton Report* 1975, 4).

Western separatism received a bit of media attention in Alberta in the spring of 1976. Dr. J. Donnovan Ross, a former provincial Social Credit cabinet minister, publicly advocated separatism. He proposed that the western provinces form a Commonwealth of Western Canada with former Alberta premier (and a senator by that time) Ernest Manning as interim prime minister. Manning was publicly opposed to separatism, however, and nothing came of Ross's efforts (*St. John's Edmonton Report* 1976, 13-14).

Separatism was not taking hold in Alberta. In July 1978, Victoria, BC lawyer Douglas Christie came to hold a series of meetings in Alberta on behalf of his BC-based organization, the Committee of Western Independence. He was hoping to generate sales of memberships in the Committee. His efforts were supported by the WNA, which was close to fading from the scene. When asked about WNA membership in northern Alberta, local WNA leader Doug Low replied, "it's a joke." The WNA's executive director, Gerry Ronayne, was a little more optimistic about the prospects for support for the organization. But Christie's meetings were poorly attended; "in Calgary, the group drew a total of 50 to three meetings" (*Saint John's Edmonton Report* 1978b, 15).

During 1979, with Joe Clark as prime minister, conflict between the

Alberta and Ontario governments over energy policy and oil pricing was really heating up. Albertans were becoming increasingly concerned that they were going to continue to be exploited by central Canada. Attitudes were hardening. Roy Farran, former solicitor general in Peter Lougheed's government, spoke for many Albertans when he wrote, "Ontario wants our money. Ontario wants our oil for as close to nothing as it can get it. And Ontario can go to hell" (*Alberta Report* 1979a, 14).

The polarization on oil pricing was preparing the ground for the rise of Alberta separatism. As *Alberta Report* noted, "a great many people" in Alberta felt the province was getting a raw deal. "And the kind of unilateral resource plunder that eastern citizens are suggesting would convert them overnight into a separatist movement that would make the Quebec phenomenon look like the pee wee league" (*Alberta Report* 1979a, 16). Clearly, the stage was being set.

A few weeks later, in the fall of 1979, Peter Lougheed spoke at a fundraising dinner in Edmonton. About a thousand PC supporters were in attendance. Lougheed gave a strong defence of Alberta's position in the energy war:

> The tone of the message was defiance. What remained of Alberta's rapidly vanishing conventional oil reserves, he said, was not going to be sold off at far *less* than the world price to a province that for a hundred years had been selling almost everything it produces at far *more* than the world price. Everywhere in the room people rose to their feet. The applause was loud, sustained, vigorous. Hands were high and thrust forward towards the speaker. It meant more than mere approval. They were urging him on (Byfield 1979c, 20).

Most Albertans were firmly behind the premier, and there was an atmosphere of defiance towards Ottawa and the central Canadian provinces. Tension was increasing.

ALBERTA REPORT, THE ALBERTA PRESS, AND THE EAST-WEST CONFLICT

Alberta Report magazine was an unabashed defender of Alberta and its oil industry. It would be hard to imagine any publication doing a better job than *Alberta Report* did on behalf of Alberta. And the magazine was up front about its allegiances.

Alberta Report took shape as the result of combining two other sister publications, *Saint John's Edmonton Report* and *Saint John's Calgary Report* in September 1979. In his editorial announcing the creation of *Alberta Report*, Ted Byfield ends as follows:

> Above all we must tell the Alberta story from an unsuspect Alberta viewpoint. We are almost the only Alberta news publication whose ownership lies within the province. In any future changes we are resolved that ownership will remain here. We feel that at this time, more than at any time in her history, Alberta needs its own voice. We will presume to provide it (Byfield 1979b, 1).

Provide it they did.

Not only did *Alberta Report* provide Alberta's voice, it also reminded readers on a regular basis that most of the other media in Alberta were "branch plants" of eastern companies. And those other media outlets reflected the views of their eastern masters rather than the interests of their Alberta readers or viewers. Indeed, the magazine's cover story for its July 13, 1979 issue was "Alberta's branch office press." The article's subtitle was "The West's mighty publishers have vanished and the East has taken over" (*Saint John's Report* 1979, 18).

The implications of eastern ownership were not hard to discern, and Ted Byfield made them as plain as day for his readers.

In March 1979, Alberta's provincial election resulted in Peter Lougheed's Progressive Conservative Party winning 74 of the 79 legislative seats. Thus the opposition in the Legislature would be very small, and likely not very effective. As a result, Patrick O'Callaghan, publisher of the *Edmonton Journal*, declared that his newspaper would provide the needed political opposition, since not enough non-Tory MLAs had been elected.

Ted Byfield then pointed out what this would mean from a pro-Alberta perspective:

[T]he newspaper which now proclaims itself as the Lougheed government's opposition is in a real sense not an Alberta newspaper at all. Like almost every other daily paper in the province, it is owned in Toronto. Its publisher is appointed from Toronto. Its editor is appointed from Toronto. Its senior management reports to Toronto and Toronto decides whether they have done a good or bad job. Its future is decided in Toronto, and its profits, which are drawn from Alberta and are enormous, flow wherever Toronto wants them to flow, usually eastward. We remember of course that the declared purpose of the Lougheed government is to correct the historical weakness of Canada by shifting the centre of its economic power westward, i.e. away from Toronto. That this branch office operation in Edmonton should now be assigned the task of opposing such a government is hardly therefore surprising (Byfield 1979a, 1).

A few months later, in the fall of 1979, Premier Lougheed gave a speech in Vancouver presenting Alberta's case for receiving the world price for its oil. Alberta's major newspapers largely disapproved of the speech, and *Alberta Report* carried an article describing those papers' responses. The article made it clear that these were not really Alberta newspapers as can be seen from the following excerpts:

The *Edmonton Journal* (head office, 321 Bloor St. E., Toronto) was appalled....

"The premier's methods," said the Calgary *Albertan*, (head office, 444 Front St. W., Toronto), "leave more than a little to be desired...."

"Time to cool it, Peter," said a headline over editor Ron Collister's column in the *Edmonton Sun* (head office, 333 King Street E., Toronto) (*Alberta Report* 1979b, 13).

Alberta's Toronto-owned press did not appear very willing to support Alberta's interests.

There was one notable and brief exception to this pattern, however. Early in 1981, when separatist sentiment in Alberta was red-hot, Patrick O'Callaghan gave a very pro-Alberta speech that received considerable attention. In 1979, he had declared his paper to be Lougheed's opposition, but by early 1981, he was much more amenable to the premier's pro-Alberta stance. Speaking to the Scandinavian Club in Edmonton he said:

> What you see now in Alberta is a province earnestly searching for an identity that might well be available to it only outside Canada. It is looking for a leader to give separatism legitimacy and the man it wants is Peter Lougheed ...If Alberta loses the power struggle with Ottawa on energy, the separatists might well get the leader they hunger for ...The final option for Alberta is not a weak caving-in to federal peace terms, but separation ...When the guns open up, there can be no surrender. Alberta has clearly dug itself in too deeply to retreat and the majority of Albertans are down there in the trenches with their government (*Alberta Report* 1981, 3).

A number of public officials, including federal Energy Minister Marc Lalonde, openly condemned O'Callaghan's speech.

A few months later, however, Ted Byfield had a reason once again to remind his readers that the *Edmonton Journal* and the *Calgary Herald* were run from Toronto. Those papers, as well as many others across Canada, were owned by Southam Company. The Southam papers all carried a Saturday supplement called *Today Magazine* which in one issue published a cartoon making fun of Alberta oilmen. Byfield viewed the cartoon as an expression of "regional resentment in its rawest form." He went on to point out that "All three Canadian newspaper chains are run from Toronto. All three television networks are run from Toronto.... The whole country is thereby force-fed the Toronto prejudice" (Byfield 1981, 52).

In 1986, *Alberta Report* branched out by starting *Western Report* and including more non-Alberta western content in the magazine. Byfield explained that with the end of Alberta's economic boom, the magazine had to expand into a larger market if it wished to survive. So it would, henceforth, defend a united western viewpoint as the other media would not defend the western view. "Every major western newspaper is owned in Toronto. All can be counted on to oppose any movement towards any unification of outlook in the West" (T. Byfield 1986, 52).

Alberta Report was the print media voice of the pro-Alberta movement, and most of the other print media in the province were the "branch plant press." The magazine's main audience segments were (arguably) pro-West regionalist elements and social conservatives who loved its defence of traditional morality. Without conflict between Ottawa and Alberta, however, the pro-Alberta market segment became soft and dissipated, leaving a social conservative support base. But the social conservatives were not numerous enough to keep the magazine afloat, and after becoming a national publication called *The Report*, in 1999, it folded in 2003.

Perhaps *Alberta Report* was a victim of its own success. The magazine so powerfully articulated Alberta's case that many Alberta citizens resolved never to be trampled on by the federal government again. They became active and vocal in defending Alberta's rightful place in Canada. *Alberta Report* certainly helped in the founding and early success of the Reform Party, and the Reform Party made central Canada and the federal Liberals sit up and take notice. Something like the NEP could no longer be implemented once a western-rights party had taken hold in the West.

Although Ottawa still annoys Alberta, it hasn't, in years, proposed the kind of rip-offs favoured by Pierre Trudeau. For that, *Alberta Report* likely deserves plenty of credit.

PETER LOUGHEED
ON *ALBERTA REPORT*

On the occasion of *Alberta Report*'s 25th anniversary, former premier Peter Lougheed wrote of his appreciation for the magazine's support of his government, in its struggles with Ottawa. *Alberta Report* was very critical of the Lougheed government's policies in other areas, such as education, but it strongly supported a provincial rights perspective on issues of federalism.

As Lougheed himself put it, "on the major national issues involving Alberta ...the support by the *Alberta Report* was strong and its impact was very significant and positive" (Lougheed 1999, 12). This was most obvious regarding the NEP, which he calls "the most extreme attack on the ownership of resource rights of the province that could possibly be envisioned" (Lougheed 1999, 12).

 In the early days of the NEP, when the Alberta government responded by curtailing oil shipments to eastern Canada, the magazine defended the province. "Week after week the *Alberta Report* made it clear to Albertans, and also to Canadians, that the federal government was attempting to destroy the right of ownership of oil and gas by Albertans" (Lougheed 1999, 12). And this was noticed by the federal government, for as Lougheed says, "we discovered many Ottawa politicians, bureaucrats and journalists at the time were reading the magazine intensely, and collectively coming to the conclusion that Albertans were united in taking such a strong stand against this attack upon their resources" (Lougheed 1999, 12).

It's clear that *Alberta Report* was a force to be reckoned with in the conflict with Trudeau and his henchmen. The magazine was never a mouthpiece for the provincial government – indeed, it forcefully opposed the Alberta government on a number of issues. But it was a powerful opponent of socialism and federal intrusion into the affairs of Alberta.

CONCLUSION

The Alberta separatist movement began to take shape during the 1970s. Pierre Trudeau can take much credit for that. His policy of official bilingualism upset many Albertans and other westerners. But it was his policies on energy and oil pricing that really got the ball rolling.

The IAA was formed in 1974, largely by Calgary oilmen. It was a small group, but it had high calibre leadership. With men such as John Rudolph and Milt Harradence involved, the IAA arguably had the best leadership of any separatist organization ever in Alberta. The irony is that they were gone before the fun really started in 1980. Lack of credible leadership would plague the separatist movement throughout the subsequent decade.

Towards the end of the 1970s, tension between Alberta and central Canada was building. Support for separatism was negligible, but Albertans were becoming increasingly concerned about losing their non-renewable oil and gas resources at prices far below the world price, due to federal policies. As the champion of Alberta's position, Peter Lougheed received tremendous support from most Albertans.

But Alberta's position was about to become even more precarious. With the fall of Joe Clark's minority government, in December 1979, and the February 1980 federal election, events were coming to a head. The re-emergence of Pierre Trudeau as prime minister, and his social-istic drive to seize control of Alberta's oil and gas industry, became the torch that lit the separatist fuse.

REFERENCES

Alberta Report. 1979a. "The ugly Albertan." September 14: 14-16.

Alberta Report. 1979b. "A word from the branch offices." November 16: 13.

Alberta Report Supplement. 1979. "Alberta vs. Ottawa." *The Search for Oil & Gas*. November 30: 1-5.

Alberta Report. 1981. "Ottawa's Irish irritant." February 6: 2-5.

Anderson, Owen. 1971. "The Unfinished Revolt." In *The Unfinished Revolt: Some Views on Western Independence*, eds. John J. Barr and Owen Anderson. Toronto: McClelland and Stewart Limited, 35-59.

Barr, John J. 1971. "Beyond Bitterness: The New Western Radicalism." In *The Unfinished Revolt: Some Views on Western Independence*, eds. John J. Barr and Owen Anderson. Toronto: McClelland and Stewart Limited, 11-32.

Blackman, W. 1974. *The Cost of Confederation: An Analysis of Costs to Alberta Part I (Economic Activity)*. Calgary: Independent Alberta Association.

Boothroyd, Peter. 1971. "Independence For Whom?" In *The Unfinished Revolt: Some Views on Western Independence*, eds. John J. Barr and Owen Anderson. Toronto: McClelland and Stewart Limited, 135-143.

Byfield, Ted. 1979a. "The Fat Cat Puppet of Toronto." *Saint John's Edmonton Report*. April 6: 1.

Byfield, Ted. 1979b. "Alberta Report." *Alberta Report.* September 7: 1.

Byfield, Ted. 1979c. "Why Such Vigorous Applause?" *Alberta Report.* November 9: 20.

Byfield, Ted. 1982. "Take it and grin, Alberta, thanks to the Southam Co." *Alberta Report.* January 11: 52.

Byfield, Ted. 1986. "Why Southam's branch office fears a trend to western unity." *Alberta Report.* June 16: 52.

Evans, C. D. 2001. *Milt Harradence: The Western Flair.* Calgary: Durance Vile Publications.

Hollinshead, Michael J., and W. Blackman. 1975. *The Cost of Confederation: An Analysis of Costs to Alberta Part II (Inter Governmental Transfer of Funds).* Calgary: Independent Alberta Association.

Koch, George. 2003. "Even before the NEP, the separatist siren beckons." In *Lougheed & the War With Ottawa 1971-1984 (Alberta in the 20th Century Volume 11),* ed. Paul Bunner. Edmonton: History Book Publications Ltd.

Lougheed, Peter. 1974. "Fueling the Feud." *Maclean's.* February: 20, 62-63.

Lougheed, Peter. 1999. "A voice hard to ignore." *Alberta Report.* January 11: 12.

Love, James. 1971. "Alberta in the Financial Vise." In *The Unfinished Revolt: Some Views on Western Independence,* eds. John J. Barr and Owen Anderson. Toronto: McClelland and Stewart Limited, 105-116.

Ludwig, Jack. 1975. "The Seventies belong to Lougheed." *Maclean's.* July: 19-23.

McDonald, Patrick N. 1975. *The Juridical Nature of Canadian Federalism: The Status of A Province.* Calgary: Independent Alberta Association.

Pratt, Larry and Garth Stevenson. 1981. "Introduction." In *Western Separatism: The Myths, Realities & Dangers,* eds. Larry Pratt and Garth Stevenson. Edmonton: Hurtig Publishers.

Saint John's Edmonton Report. 1974. "The unthinkable would work, experts say, in $40,000 study of 'independent' Alberta." December 2: 25-28.

St. John's Edmonton Report. 1975. "No chance seen for separatist success, university study shows." March 17: 3-4.

St. John's Edmonton Report. 1976. "A Socred sees separation as West's answer." May 3: 13-14.

Saint John's Edmonton Report. 1977a. "A Low voice for western independence." March 7: 10-11.

Saint John's Edmonton Report. 1977b. "Do Albertans really feel alienated from the eastern Canadians? Prof's study show they sure do and people over 35 are worst." March 7: 11-12.

Saint John's Edmonton Report. 1977c. "Nationalists woo Horner." April 11: 18.

Saint John's Edmonton Report. 1978a. "Tired of the hassle, the independent Mr. Rudolph heads south." February 13: 24.

Saint John's Edmonton Report. 1978b. "Western nationalists mount their crusade; even if they don't care about it in this town." July 21: 15.

Saint John's Report. 1979. "Alberta's branch office press." July 13: 18-21.

Stewart, Walter. 1969. "The Coming Showdown With the West." *Maclean's.* July: 34-35,37, 39-40.

Wood, David G. 1985. *The Lougheed Legacy.* Toronto: Key Porter Books Limited.

CHAPTER 3

THE NATIONAL ENERGY PROGRAM AND THE EXPLOSION OF SEPARATISM

As Canada entered the 1980s, the country was in the midst of a federal election campaign, and the stakes were particularly high for Alberta. The Liberals under their resurrected leader, Pierre Trudeau, were running on a platform of obtaining cheap Alberta oil for the benefit of central Canada. When the Liberals won the election, Albertans knew that bad times were just around the corner.

Some Albertans began to attend separatist meetings, and the separatist movement grew in anticipation of Trudeau's expected raid on Alberta's oil industry. When that raid finally arrived in the form of the NEP, thousands of Albertans became seriously interested in separatism. For many, Alberta could only free itself from the clutches of Trudeau's socialistic tyranny by becoming independent.

Many observers noted, however, that the movement lacked credible leadership. That was the major factor holding the separatist movement back. It was a problem that the movement was never able to finally overcome.

THE 1980 FEDERAL ELECTION

In May 1979, a federal election was held and the federal PCs formed a minority government headed by Joe Clark. However, in December of that year, Clark's minority government fell when it lost a House of Commons vote on its proposed budget. An election was scheduled for February 1980. The price of energy, and a proposed eighteen-cents-a-gallon gasoline tax, in particular, were the major reasons the opposition parties defeated the government. In Ontario, some politicians proclaimed that Clark's budget represented a "sellout to Alberta."

The 1980 federal election campaign was like no other election campaign. The Liberals decided to run on an explicitly anti-Alberta platform, playing off one part of the country against the other. By winning most of the seats in Ontario and Quebec, they could easily form the government. They didn't need any seats in the West, especially Alberta.

Despite resigning as Liberal leader in November 1979, the surprise fall of Clark's government convinced Pierre Trudeau to remain as the party leader after all. One rally early in the campaign gave a clear indication of the major issue:

> Mr. Trudeau shared the stage with Ontario Liberal leader Stuart Smith in Toronto's Royal York Hotel. Before 450 cheering Grits, Dr. Smith unleashed a vitriolic tirade against the supposed avarice of oil-producing Alberta. "Peter Lougheed has to realize that he cannot be a member of Canada and OPEC at the same time," he declared, as Mr. Trudeau sat in silence. In this way the Liberals revealed their main strategy: To win the federal election in Ontario by blaming Alberta

36

for excessive energy costs. But the chief vote-getter would be the outspoken Dr. Smith. Mr. Trudeau would say nothing, lest threats to provincial rights aggravate Quebec. Thus the Liberal Party of Canada delivered itself into the hands of its most radical element, the Ontario provincial leadership, for the purposes of winning an election and, in effect, determining a policy which could lead to the end of confederation (*Alberta Report* 1980a, 9).

The effect of such a campaign for Alberta was unmistakable. As Ted Byfield put it, "No previous federal election has ever been so decisive to the future of this province" (Byfield 1980a, 44).

Right from the beginning of the campaign, the Liberals were well ahead in all of the opinion polls, and this remained the case. As the February 18 election date drew near, *Alberta Report* warned "that if Mr. Trudeau is elected, as all the polls insist he will be, a major confrontation between Alberta and Ottawa will immediately ensue" (*Alberta Report* 1980b, 10). And this would be no ordinary political dispute because this "confrontation will surely test the fabric of confederation" (*Alberta Report* 1980b, 12).

The Liberals won a majority government on February 18, with 2 MPs from Manitoba and none from the other 3 western provinces. There was widespread anger in Alberta and separation immediately became a hot topic in the province. Stanley Roberts, the president of the prestigious Canada West Foundation, sized up the situation saying, "given a Rene Levesque calibre leader, today's embryonic separatist sentiment could mushroom into a formidable and destructive power" (Roberts 1980, 10).

Ted Byfield wrote a powerful column about the results of the election and the consequences for Alberta:

> The people of central Canada have now served notice upon the west that if it does not sell what's left of its most valuable asset at something close to half price, then they will elect a government that is committed to move in and seize it. That is the meaning to Albertans of last week's general election (Byfield 1980b, 44).

And he closed the column with a very ominous exhortation, stating,

> each of us within his soul must make a decision. No one
> wants the country split. The west wants to be Canadian.
> But do we want to be Canadian at any price? My own
> answer is no. The day the Central Canada Party, what
> was once called the Liberal Party, gains passage of a bill
> to seize the west's oil resources is the day that I cease to
> consider myself Canadian (Byfield 1980b, 44).

That was pretty strong stuff and *Alberta Report* subsequently received a number of letters from people concerned that it had turned separatist. To answer this concern Ted Byfield wrote another column in which he asked, "Is *Alberta Report* in favour of separatism? Certainly not" (Byfield 1980c, 52).

A few days following the election, Doug Christie founded a new organization (with an old name) in BC called the Western National Association (WNA). In March he spoke at the Hotel Macdonald in Edmonton and 120 people attended the meeting. He made it clear that the organization was completely opposed to western Canada joining the United States, saying, "I would never replace an alien, overbearing centralist bureaucracy 3,000 miles away for an even more alien, more centralist, more overbearing bureaucracy 5,000 miles away" (*Alberta Report* 1980c, 11).

Christie's WNA quickly descended into internal squabbling. He then left the group and formed the WCC, in June. During the summer he held more meetings in Alberta. Twenty-five people attended in Medicine Hat, 55 in Edmonton, and 275 showed up in Lethbridge (Harrington 1981, 28). Clearly the movement was growing.

Immediately after the February 18 election, 66-year old Edmonton businessman Elmer Knutson wrote a letter to the editor of the *Edmonton Journal*. It appeared in the paper on February 22, and received considerable attention. He argued that Quebec had taken over the country: "Let us then look at the Canada of February 19, 1980, the day that will be remembered as the day after the second battle of the plains of Abraham, when the Anglophones lost and the French won" (Harrington 1981, 25). He then said Canada must "divorce" Quebec. "The divorce must be done now or else Western Canada, from the Ontario and Manitoba border, must separate physically as we did politically last night, February 18th, 1980" (Harrington 1981, 25).

Knutson's letter to the editor generated immediate response, and he claimed to have received 3,800 letters and phone calls of support. Due to this support, a meeting was held and an organization was formed with Knutson as its leader. It was called West-Fed, or the Western Canadian Federation, and it was incorporated on May 23, 1980 (Harrington 1981, 25).

West-Fed advocated the formation of a federation of the western provinces. In this respect it was "separatist" because the federation would be a separate country from Canada. However, Knutson always rejected the term "separatist" for himself and for West-Fed. He had a peculiar view that the 1931 Statute of Westminster had made each of Canada's provinces sovereign, and therefore Canada as a political unit did not legally exist. The provinces were free to federate as Canada, or remain independent. But because Canada as an actual political unit did not legally exist, there was nothing to "separate" from. Thus he was not a separatist as far as he was concerned. This was a rather subtle distinction that most people appear to have missed. West-Fed was widely regarded as a separatist organization.

During the summer of 1980, West-Fed held a number of meetings, mostly in rural Alberta. Knutson was the featured speaker and would often draw crowds of 200 to 300 people (Harrington 1981, 27). In September, West-Fed held a meeting in Red Deer attended by 600 people. The organization claimed at this point to be selling about 300 memberships per week (*Alberta Report* 1980e, 6). The organization appeared to be growing rapidly.

The growth of separatist sentiment in Alberta was being noticed by others. The leader of the Alberta Liberal Party, Nick Taylor, was warning his fellow Liberals not to provoke Albertans. He said that any move by the federal government to control Alberta's oil "would be tantamount to the Boston tea party or the first shot at Fort Sumter and would turn every westerner into a separatist" (*Alberta Report* 1980d, 4). And early in October, a couple of weeks before the federal budget was to be announced, Stan Roberts of the Canada West Foundation stated that "right now western Canada has a higher level of disaffection for the rest of Canada than Quebec ever had" (*Alberta Report* 1980f, 7).

THE NATIONAL ENERGY PROGRAM
AND ITS EFFECTS ON ALBERTA

In the lead up to the federal government's October 28 budget, indications of what that budget may contain were causing anxiety and anger in Alberta. It was expected that the federal government would impose new taxes on oil and natural gas, and perhaps take even more extreme measures to control Alberta's oil industry. *Alberta Report* was predicting "economic civil war within Canada" (*Alberta Report* 1980g, 2).

Beforehand, Premier Lougheed booked time slots on a number of Alberta television stations, in order to give Alberta's response to the anticipated budget. Polls showed that support for separatism among Albertans had jumped from 10% to 20% in the preceding six months. When asked about the prospects for western separatism, Prime Minister Trudeau replied, "The chances of western separatism are nil and non-existent" (*Alberta Report* 1980g, 2).

On October 28, Finance Minister Allan MacEachen announced the federal government's new budget before the House of Commons. Accompanying the federal budget, Energy Minister Marc Lalonde introduced the government's new energy policy, the infamous NEP. The effect of these two policies:

> was to supplant the provincial authority with the federal in the energy field, to gradually oust American companies, and at the same time to strangle Canadian independents through lack of cash. This would pave the way, oil men predicted, for a gigantic take-over of production facilities by the government-owned Petro-Canada, in other words for the gradual socialization of the most free enterprise major industry in the economy (*Alberta Report* 1980h, 2).

Alberta Report said that October 28, 1980 "will no doubt go down as the darkest day in Alberta history" (*Alberta Report* 1980h, 2).

Two days later, Premier Lougheed gave an evening television address to the people of Alberta, outlining the province's response. Alberta was going to cut back oil shipments to central Canada in three stages, beginning February 1, 1981. Once the third stage kicked in, the total cutback amount would be 180,000 barrels per day. Alberta was also going to delay approval for two oil sands plants and launch a court challenge to a federal tax on natural gas:

> "I think that what's happened," he said, "is that the Ottawa government has, without negotiation, without agreement, simply walked into our home and occupied the livingroom ...I don't think we can turn our backs on the pioneers and forefathers who fought to have resource ownership rights for the people of Alberta." Therefore, "this is not a fight between Peter and Pierre." It is "Albertans deciding whether they want more and more of their lives controlled by the federal government" (*Alberta Report* 1980h, 2).

"As Lougheed spoke," *Maclean's* magazine noted, "up to 40 shoppers crowded around 13 television sets in Woodward's downtown Edmonton department store, some applauding, in a scene reminiscent of the Cuban missile crisis" (Lewis 1980, 30). Indeed, this was very much a crisis, and many Albertans were ready for a fight.

Most Albertans were angry. They felt like they were under attack from Trudeau's government, and with good reason. As usual, Ted Byfield articulated the sharpest perspective on the new energy policy:

> History will one day record that it was on Tuesday, October 28, 1980, that a government of Canada by act of deliberate policy tried to destroy the prosperity of the one section of the country that had escaped the recession and offered the best hope for the whole nation's future. At the same time it indentured the country to the Middle East's oil producers and brought its own oil industry to a catastrophic halt. Historians will be hard pressed to find anywhere an act of government so irresponsible, so vindictive and so insane as that which was produced last week by Mr. Trudeau and his thugs

41

at Ottawa (Byfield 1980e, 60).

Referring repeatedly in this piece to the Trudeau Liberals as "thugs," Byfield explained the two reasons for the new federal government policy:

> The purpose of the budget was simply to pay off Ontario and Quebec at the expense of the western provinces. But beyond this there is another reason, one that seethes in the heart of Pierre Trudeau. People say that he is indifferent to western Canada, and this may once have been true. I think it is true no longer. He now has a keen feeling about us because we have so long and so decisively told him that we want neither him nor the gang of toadies around him. For this he now hates us, and passionately. It is a hatred that runs to the roots of the man's being. It is the hatred of the socialist for the individualist, the cold fear of the high-born for the self-made, the aversion of the theorist for the pragmatist, the derision of the urbanist for the peasant, the disdain of the intellectual for the uncouth, the contempt of the Gaul for the Slav. All these hatreds have helped to dictate the posture of the Trudeau government towards the West, and on Tuesday, the 28th of October, they were paraded before the nation in the form of public policy (Byfield 1980e, 60).

Following the introduction of the NEP, there was an immediate jump in support for separatism in Alberta. A Southam poll found that 23% of those surveyed supported separatism. Prof. Warren Blackman of the University of Calgary predicted that western Canada would separate within the decade. But Trudeau dismissed any western concerns about the loss of resources as "hysteria." And he warned westerners, "If you try to get anything under threat of separatism my answer will be no" (*Alberta Report* 1980i, 12-13).

But the fun was only just beginning. "All over the province, at meetings, on radio and television shows, in beer parlors and board rooms, and in the headlines of daily newspapers, the vision of a western Canadian independent nation spread like a prairie fire" (*Alberta Report*

1980j, 12). Some prominent citizens came out publicly in favour of separatism. The most prominent was Carl Nickle, a former PC MP from Calgary. He joined West-Fed and began speaking on behalf of that organization. Stanley Milner, president of Chieftain Developments, said that separatism is "like a prairie fire. If you had a powerful leader – for instance, Peter Lougheed – the business community would be behind you" (*Alberta Report* 1980j, 12). In a Senate speech, Senator Ernest Manning (former long-time Alberta premier) warned about the separatist threat saying:

> I am deeply troubled by the large number of serious-minded responsible people in western Canada who a year ago would have rejected the idea of separation out of hand but who are now joining or supporting organizations advocating that the West separate. Such organizations are attracting members and fringe supporters not by the hundreds but by the thousands (*Alberta Report* 1980j, 12).

A novelty industry of separatist gimmicks also sprang up, with t-shirts and hats bearing phrases like "Republic of Alberta," and other similar concepts.

Separatist meetings began to be held around the province. The largest separatist meeting in the history of western Canada was held November 20, 1980, at Edmonton's Jubilee Auditorium. It was organized by Doug Christie who was also the main speaker. Christie had challenged any politician to debate him, and the only one to accept the challenge was Alberta Liberal Party leader Nick Taylor. Attendance at the meeting was estimated to be between 2500 and 2700.

Christie delivered a passionate plea for western independence after reciting the many reasons for western dissatisfaction with Canada. Taylor was shouted down by the crowd. He told them they were "greedy" and were being manipulated by Lougheed and BC Premier Bill Bennett (Harrington 1981, 30).

West-Fed also had some large meetings. At a November meeting in Airdrie, 425 to 450 people came to hear Knutson, former Edmonton alderman Robert Matheson and University of Calgary economist Warren Blackman. Blackman stated that Trudeau's "centralist socialism" was incompatible with the West's "free enterprise zeal" (*Alberta Report* 1980k, 3).

But the big West-Fed draw was Carl Nickle. As a well-known multi-millionaire and philanthropist, he drew a "blue-chip" audience of over 800 people to a luncheon in Calgary:

> In Calgary, the reasoned speech of oilman Carl Nickle was interrupted 25 times by the applause and cheering of businessmen who jammed the back of the hall and spilled out the door into the lobby. The West is an economic colony and can face that situation in three ways, said the owner of Conventures Limited. "We can lie down, take it and be stomped upon; a decision few would accept. We can continue seeking a reasonable compromise, as for example Alberta Premier Peter Lougheed still seeks. Or we can opt for a separate Western Canada federation. Many, like myself, are not prepared to see the colonial situation (continue) over many years ahead." At the end of his speech, the business elite of Calgary rose for a long and boisterous ovation (*Alberta Report* 1980k, 3).

At one of the luncheon tables, the executives of various oil companies were asked "if everybody had heard that Kentucky Fried Chicken now has a Liberal bucket on the menu. 'All left wings and assholes,' said Petro-Info Company President Jim Thomson, and everyone laughed" (Zwarun 1980, 28).

Despite the rapid growth of the separatist movement, it continued to suffer from a lack of high calibre leadership. But there was always a possibility that such a leader could appear:

> The federalists' worst fear is that a charismatic separatist leader will emerge among the baseball caps and bumper stickers. North Vancouver-Burnaby MP Charles Cook echoes many when he says: "When we get a first-rate credible leader there will be an incredible explosion of separatism. Look out if they find a credible leader – it is the most dangerous thing going on in Canada today,

far more dangerous than Quebec because it is based on economic, not cultural, issues" (Zwarun 1980, 31).

With separatist sentiment growing by leaps and bounds, Trudeau did not appear too concerned. In fact, *Maclean's* magazine saw him as further inflaming the situation:

> Prime Minister Trudeau, in a Regina appearance last month generally described as disastrous, probably goaded hundreds into attending West-Fed meetings simply by his arrogant dismissal of separatist sentiment. "I saved Quebec," said Trudeau with a shrug. "Somebody else will have to save the West." The danger is that the messiah that might appear to save the West will lead it not back into Confederation, but into a new, free state (Zwarun 1980, 32).

A couple of weeks after the large separatist meeting in Edmonton's Jubilee Auditorium, West-Fed had a meeting in Calgary attended by 900. This was considered a disappointingly small number. A week or so later, Doug Christie's WCC held a meeting in Calgary attended by 1100 at that city's Jubilee Auditorium. This meeting was different, however. First, a phoned-in bomb threat delayed the meeting because police had to search the building to make sure it was safe. And secondly, a number of people attending this particular meeting were federalists who came to disrupt it. Shouting matches between separatists and federalists erupted before Christie spoke, and then he was continuously interrupted by hecklers. After he spoke there was a question and answer session where many federalists took the opportunity to express their views. Due to the problems at this meeting, the *Calgary Herald* suggested that the separatist movement in southern Alberta may have already been "running out of steam" (*Alberta Report* 1980n, 7-8).

Meanwhile, the NEP was having a nasty effect on the Alberta oil industry. Drilling rigs and their crews were heading south to the friendly environment of the United States. Millions of dollars worth of planned exploration in Alberta was cancelled. Exploration budgets were being slashed, and jobs were vanishing. The negative effects of the NEP were catalogued by *Alberta Report*. Ted Byfield expressed concern that Ottawa may treat other western industries the way it did the oil industry, and then asked:

> So what should we do if Ottawa persists? We have been given a final moment of calm in which to decide. For me, I have long since made up my mind. If they take the resources, we should separate. I like Canada. But I like freedom a whole lot more. I have no intention to become a Lalonde sharecropper (Byfield 1981a, 44).

Toward the end of January 1981, West-Fed held a rally at the Edmonton Jubilee Auditorium attended by 1000 people. The separatist movement was not ebbing. This was a successful meeting with a country and western band and a team of comedians. Afterwards, Elmer Knutson spoke as well as economist Warren Blackman of Calgary. But the most popular part of the meeting was an address by Peter Hemingway:

> For the West-Fed organizers, the high point of the evening was the appearance of Edmonton architect Peter Hemingway, who appealed to the crowd in an impassioned speech which would have done any evangelist proud. Mr. Hemingway, a new face on the separatist podium, has designed many of the most distinctive buildings in the provincial capital, including the Muttart Conservatory, Coronation Pool and the Pentecostal Tabernacle. As well he designed the Chinook Shopping Centre in Calgary and the County of Strathcona's fire hall and administration buildings (*Alberta Report* 1981b, 6).

Hemingway had not reached the point of outright commitment to separatism, but he was concerned about what Trudeau was up to and so was willing to speak at the West-Fed meeting (*Alberta Report* 1981b, 6).

On February 15, WCC leader Doug Christie publicly debated former Alberta MP Jack Horner at the town of Rimbey. Close to 600 people attended the debate, and the crowd was solidly behind Christie. Horner had switched from the federal PCs to the Liberals in 1977 and Trudeau had immediately rewarded him with a cabinet position. He lost his seat in the 1979 federal election, and was considered by many

46

to be a kind of traitor due to his support of the Trudeau Liberals. The crowd was unimpressed by what Horner had to say and he was shouted down by the crowd three times. Christie, on the other hand, received a standing ovation for verbally blasting Trudeau and calling for western separation (*Alberta Report* 1981c, 6).

As the time of Alberta's first oil cutback approached, the federal government went on a propaganda campaign to turn public opinion against Alberta. Because less under-priced Alberta oil would be available, eastern Canada would have to import extra foreign oil at the world price. To cover the extra cost, the federal government implemented a half-cent per litre tax on gasoline. Marc Lalonde called this tax the "Lougheed levy." A day after the levy announcement, the federal Consumer Affairs Office released a report saying that oil companies had overcharged Canadians about $12 billion through price fixing. Alberta was blamed as "the key" to this rip-off (Hopkins 1981, 2).

With Alberta's oil cutbacks beginning to take effect, there was some fear that Ottawa would exercise its "declaratory powers," whereby the federal government could seize control of Alberta's oil resources. The declaratory powers were reserved for the federal government in the BNA Act for emergency situations (Hopkins 1981, 6).

Ted Byfield pointed out that the Consumer Affairs Office report attacking the oil industry was very unfair. Under the law the industry could not be convicted of anything. That is, there had been no crime. Trudeau thus resorted to a different mechanism to punish it:

> So whatever the law might say, and whatever further
> steps might still be taken, the industry has already been
> found guilty. It has been tried, convicted and publicly
> blackguarded, all by bureaucrats. No rules of evidence,
> no privilege of counsel, no due process of trial, no cross-
> examination, nothing. That is our "rights" champion's
> latest contribution to democracy in Canada (Byfield
> 1981b, 52).

What happened was that "Big Oil was singled out for special prosecution secretly and outside the law. We now have trial by Trudeau bureaucrat for those in disfavour with Ottawa" (Byfield 1981b, 52).

Early in March, West-Fed held a meeting in Edmonton where the speaker was Dr. Ruth Gorman, a former adviser to Prime Minister John Diefenbaker. She had helped in the writing of Diefenbaker's Bill of Rights as well as in achieving the franchise for Canada's First Nations peoples. Dr. Gorman was very concerned that the Trudeau government's constitutional proposals were going to be harmful to the West. Her biggest concern was the failure to include property rights in the constitution. That, combined with the proposal to entrench equalization payments in the constitution could lead to the West losing control of its resources. As she put it, if the Trudeau government got its way, she feared that "neither we (westerners) nor the provinces have any right to hang onto either the land or its revenue. We have lost them" (*Alberta Report* 1981e, 3).

Later in the same month, however, things turned bad for West-Fed. The entire Calgary region executive, including its president Donald Noyes and communications director Michael Byfield (son of *Alberta Report* publisher Ted Byfield), resigned. They were upset by Knutson's leadership style, his penchant for making racially insensitive comments, and his public estimates of West-Fed membership figures that could not be substantiated (*Alberta Report* 1981f, 4). The Calgary office was also closed.

The dissention with Knutson decimated the Calgary organization of West-Fed. When its Calgary region annual meeting was held shortly after the executive quit, only about two dozen people showed up. The Edmonton region president and vice-president also quit, and the Red Deer region president, Howard Thompson, was considering resigning as well. All the resignations were due to opposition to Knutson's leadership (*Alberta Report* 1981g, 6-7).

In May, the Canada West Foundation released the results of a poll showing that 49% of Albertans believed their province would be just as well off as an independent country. However, only 15% of respondents actually wanted Alberta to separate from Canada. Shortly after the poll was released, West-Fed held a fund-raising barbecue in Calgary that was attended by about 200 people. That was half the number that was expected for the event. One of the speakers for the event was former

Conservative MP Stan Schumacher. He urged the audience to support Premier Lougheed. In his view, West-Fed was "a legitimate way of demonstrating to Ottawa that we're not prepared to accept everything they throw at us." Jock Andrew, the author of a book called *Bilingual Today, French Tomorrow*, and economist Warren Blackman also spoke at the event (*Alberta Report* 1981h, 6). But this meeting was a far cry from the large meetings that had been common for West-Fed just a few months earlier.

When asked about the rapid decline of West-Fed, Dr. David Elton, then president of the Canada West Foundation, blamed the organization's leadership. He said it had lumped too many issues together with western alienation, such as opposition to the metric system, and that the anti-French literature it produced was offensive. As well, it had failed to offer its membership opportunities to participate in constructive activities. The West-Fed leadership, he said, "have destroyed the political base they might otherwise have had" (*Alberta Report* 1981h, 6).

With West-Fed and other separatist meetings becoming less frequent and having substantially smaller crowds, at least one knowledgeable observer wrote that by the spring of 1981, Alberta separatism "appeared to be dying a slow, natural death" (Harrington 1981, 44).

Even with the separatist movement in disarray, however, Alberta continued to suffer from the effects of the NEP. Ted Byfield described the effects of what he called "this maniacal NEP":

> [T]he NEP after seven months has managed to cripple the Canadian exploration industry and to drive it out of the country, to increase Canadian oil consumption, to disrupt the supply of existing oil, to ship millions upon millions of dollars overseas, to jeopardize relations with the Americans, to expose us far more to dependence on Arab oil, to halt development of the tar sands, to throw federal-provincial relations into a chaos bordering on legal civil war, and to find no oil. All that in seven months! (Byfield 1981d, 52).

Although the separatist movement seemed to be faltering, the conditions that pushed people towards the movement were as bad as ever. The potential was still there. West-Fed was in an irreversible decline, but the Alberta wing of the WCC was just warming up. Once it got better organized, it would reach greater heights of success than West-Fed.

SEPARATISM AND "DISLOYALTY" TO CANADA

Separatists were faced with the accusation of being disloyal to their country. Canada was their country, so supporting Alberta's independence was an attack on that country and thus constituted disloyalty.

Related to this was the broader concept that regionalism itself was a threat to national loyalty. Many Canadians, not just westerners, often appeared to be more strongly attached to their province or their region than to their country. In this line of reasoning, affection for one's region was seen as undercutting loyalty to Canada. And with certain premiers (read: Peter Lougheed) pursuing their own parochial interests, the country would be pulled apart. Thus, regionalism was a bad thing. It would lead to the break-up of Canada.

Ted Byfield offered a very different take on regionalism. In his view, regionalism was not the *cause* of the weakening of national loyalty, but instead the *result* of the weakening of national loyalty. Canada's original national identity (at least for English-speaking Canadians) was as British North America. This concept of Canada had long been under attack, even by the federal government. As it had been undermined, regional identity had taken its place:

> Canada's national loyalty never has been strong. What there was of it has been starved out of existence through neglect and irresponsibility. The regional loyalties have sprung up to fill the vacuum created by its demise. People must believe in something. For many, belief in our nationhood was simply impossible. Belief in a "homeland" was not. But the homeland meant the region (Byfield 1980d, 44).

Byfield goes on to explain the change that has taken place through reference to his own childhood. He was born and raised in Toronto. Children at the time were taught to think of themselves as "British" in some sense:

> Our flag was the Union Jack. It consisted, we were told, of three Christian symbols – the crosses of St. George, St. Andrew and St. Patrick. This evidenced that the empire was the product of Christianity, and that behind the laws of man must lie the more fundamental laws of God (Byfield 1980d, 44).

That flag, of course, was changed under Prime Minister Lester Pearson in 1965. "The Christian symbolism of the Union Jack has been replaced by the pantheistic symbolism of the sugar maple, a tree that does not grow in the West." The change in the flag was symptomatic of a larger change away from Canada's original identity. As Byfield saw it, "the land of my birth has, in a sense, vanished" (Byfield 1980d, 44).

The result of the efforts to erase Canada's historic identity was the rise of regionalism and the consequent reduction of national loyalty:

> In short, they took away a working basis of patriotism in English-speaking Canada, Britishness, and replaced it with an obvious absurdity. In desperation men's loyalties turned instead to the homeland. And the homeland is the region. But to blame regionalism for the failure of Canadian confederation would be to mistake an effect for a cause. It would be like blaming the lifeboats for the shipwreck. The passengers, by the way, will not easily give up those lifeboats (Byfield 1980d, 44).

This is a powerful line of reasoning. By pushing Canada away from its historic identity as a kind of British North America, the powers that be were leaving people little choice but to redirect their loyalties to their local communities. What else was there for them? The cultural identity of the larger community was being euthanized, and there was nothing else of substance to replace it.

This puts the loyalty/disloyalty issue into an entirely different light. By

1980, there were two Canadas, Old Canada and New Canada. One was dying and the other was emerging. Byfield was raised in, and was loyal to, Old Canada:

> The Canada I grew up in and was expected, should the occasion arise, to fight and die for, has changed so much in the past 12 years that it has effectually ceased to exist. I think of it as Old Canada, a country pulled together in the latter 19th Century by Sir John A. Macdonald and endowed with a constitution. New Canada on the other hand has been fashioned in the latter 20th Century by Mr. Trudeau, and it is about to be endowed with a constitution (Byfield 1980f, 52).

There were certain practical outworkings of the two different Canadas, and Byfield made a long list contrasting the two. Part of that list is as follows:

> Old Canada had some harsh laws but was safe to live in. New Canada has enlightened, lenient laws and is increasingly unsafe to live in. Old Canada was generally committed to the free enterprise system, modified where necessary. New Canada is increasingly committed to the socialist system, magnified where unnecessary. Old Canada met its military obligations, in fact served magnificently in two world wars. New Canada has virtually no army and has reneged on its military obligations. Old Canada was frugal and poor but paid its way. New Canada runs at a $14 billion deficit (Byfield 1980f, 52).

In a sense these seem like two very different countries. One is fading away and being replaced by the other. What role does loyalty play when the country you love disappears? Where does your loyalty go?

As Byfield pointed out, Trudeau and his ilk:

> seem to assume that the same allegiance which we all owed to the Old Canada must automatically be payable to the New. The free Westers aren't so sure about that and neither am I. When people put the question –

Are you loyal to Canada? – I have to ask: To which Canada? The one we used to know? Or the one which Mr. Trudeau is forcing upon us? I certainly felt part of the first but that country doesn't seem to be there any more. About the second I have grave doubts (Byfield 1980f, 52).

So it was not a question of being disloyal to Canada. It was a question of determining to which Canada one was loyal. The separatists, or as Byfield here calls them, "free Westers," were indeed loyal. But they were loyal to Old Canada, not New Canada.

Byfield argued that the West had to develop an alternative to the New Canada:

[I]f we do not give ourselves another option, then we are going to be plundered and oppressed by the New Trudeau Canada in ways we can scarcely imagine. Again and again it has shown its contempt for the old institutions. Everything it does bespeaks a tyranny foreign to the values which Old Canada represented. To be loyal to the one therefore means to be alien to the other (Byfield 1980f, 52).

This kind of thinking invokes a cultural component to the case for separatism. Our national identity was under assault from Trudeau. To be loyal to Trudeau's New Canada was to be a traitor to the traditional Canadian identity.

Accounts of the early years of the Alberta separatist movement often note that it frequently consisted of people fighting for lost causes – against metrification, against bilingualism, and in support of Canada's British heritage, including the monarchy. This constituted a kind of cultural/national identity component of the case for Alberta separatism. It was a defensive component, a sort of self-defence of one's national identity.

An article in *Alberta Report,* in November 1980, discussed the two main separatist leaders of the time, Doug Christie and Elmer Knutson. Although they were rivals and competitors, they held the same basic grievances against the federal government. Interestingly, the article's summary of their grievances focuses on the cultural, rather than economic, issues:

> They accuse the eastern Liberals, particularly Pierre Trudeau, of sweeping away the values they have felt to be Canadian. Commitments to NATO and NORAD have been neglected while this country befriends Russia and Cuba. In 1968 soldiers, sailors and airmen were stripped of their *espirit de corps* as [sic] were given one bland, traditionless uniform. The Queen, once a symbol of staunch monarchist values, has lost her place. The new symbol is a flag which bears a leaf not found in western Canada. While older westerners still look to British tradition, Ottawa pushes bilingualism and metrification. And finally, they say, the spirit of free enterprise is being degraded in favour of socialism (*Alberta Report* 1980l, 7).

From this perspective, the cultural issue looms large as a reason for supporting separatism. These separatists were loyal to Old Canada and were defending English-Canada's historic identity.

HU HARRIES AND THE NATIONAL PARTY

As separatism spread across Alberta, Edmonton economist Hu Harries came up with a different idea. He figured the best plan was to form a federal political party running candidates exclusively in western Canada, people who would represent the interests of western Canadians in Parliament. This, of course, is what the Reform Party of Canada proposed to do when it came together a few years later.

Harries had been the Dean of the Faculty of Commerce at the University of Alberta, and then a Liberal MP from Edmonton during Pierre Trudeau's first term as prime minister, 1968-1972. He ran for the Liberals again in the 1980 federal election, but was soon disillusioned with the anti-Alberta stance that Trudeau took upon being re-elected.

Late in 1980, Harries addressed a West-Fed rally where he said that a new western federal political party was the answer, not separation. One argument for the West staying in Canada was that, as he calculated, "it has sent enough money to eastern Canada to buy it three times over. 'We bought it, we paid for it, now let's take advantage of it'" (*Alberta Report* 1980m, 8).

Harries decided on the name National Party, but an organization in Ottawa claimed the rights to that name and was displeased at Harries' decision to use it. But he didn't care. As he put it, "I hope to annoy a lot more Ontario outfits before I'm through" (*Alberta Report* 1981d, 6).

By the end of February 1981, Harries claimed that the National Party had about 1,000 members. Furthermore, nine constituency organizations were forming in BC and five were forming in Alberta (*Alberta Report* 1981b, 6).

Harries' proposal for a western federal party attracted the attention and support of Ted Byfield. In an editorial promoting the efforts of Harries, Byfield decried the efforts of western separatists. Although he had earlier announced qualified support for separatism, the antics of some separatists seemed to have disgusted him:

> Separatism offers no hope. Not only is it unsaleable, it seems to attract unto itself a racism that is both morally wrong and historically ignorant. No group on the prairies has been more ill used by central Canada than have our western French Canadians by the province of Quebec. Yet they become the butt of this racism and that is unconscionable (Byfield 1981c, 52).

The National Party was a rational option for westerners who were disgruntled by the federal government, but who also opposed separatism. At that point it looked like the Liberals and PCs would split the country in the next federal election, with the Liberals once again taking Quebec and the PCs dominating Ontario. If this were the case, "a 30- or 40-seat bloc from the West would inevitably hold the balance of power between them. That way it could barter its support to either party, and gain for the West those policies of government which otherwise we will simply never achieve" (Byfield 1981c, 52).

Byfield pointed out that Harries was "much deplored in conventional political circles.":

The NDP dislike him because he is an economist who is not left-wing. He is very much a free enterpriser, who runs a cattle business, a trucking business, and the best known consulting firm in the West. He even qualifies under Jack Horner's odd criterion for the true westerner. He can not only ride a horse; he is one of the most accomplished horsemen in Alberta. The Tories hate him because he ran three times for the Grits. He served one term and quit in disgust because, he said, the Liberal establishment is incapable of even considering western interests. He ran again because he believed one of Mr. Trudeau's early 'seventies recantations towards the West. He ran a third time after Mr. Trudeau promised to retire but then didn't. Finally, the Liberals hate him most of all because he has refused to go along with the farce of their much proclaimed "concern" for western problems and has become, in fact, one of their most devastating critics. He knows them inside and out (Byfield 1981c, 52).

Clearly, Byfield admired Harries and thought his National Party was a potential solution for the West's problems. Byfield asked ten of his friends what they thought of Harries' idea, and all of them said they would support it if it got off the ground.

Interestingly, one Stockwell Day of Hinton (presumably Stockwell Day, Sr.) wrote a letter to the editor to voice his disappointment with Byfield's support for Harries. Day stated his own support for separatism and concluded his letter saying, "The treachery of Trudeau, Lalonde et al, aided by the gullibility of a great many Dr. Harries, has prevailed. The break-up of Canada is fait accompli. It is over. Fini. We can't pick up all the pieces. Just one. The West" (Day 1981, 19).

The National Party did not get off the ground, and after John Turner became leader of the federal Liberal Party in 1984, Harries was back with the Liberals. He did, however, write some columns for *Alberta Report*. In one he wrote that "Alberta is being milked dry by the federal government!" (Harries 1984, 23). And when Harries died in 1986, Ted Byfield wrote a glowing three-page obituary calling Harries the "cowboy-economist" (Byfield 1986, 49).

WARREN BLACKMAN'S WEST-FED REPORT

West-Fed commissioned University of Calgary economist Warren Blackman to conduct an $8000 study of the economic basis for western alienation. The resulting report was released in August 1981. "Curiously, however, West Fed paid little heed to the document, in fact did not even send it to the newspapers" (*Alberta Report* 1981i, 2).

Blackman argued that the economic root of western alienation was "the economics of exploitation." The West was being exploited by the East. "Exploitation arises when the primary producer is paid less than what could be received in other markets. This is what economists refer to as **opportunity costs**" (Blackman 1981, 3). The West was not receiving a fair market value for some products, especially oil, and was therefore being exploited.

In order to rectify this problem, Blackman argued that westerners did not simply want "additional federal policy measures" that would give them a better deal. Instead, they wanted the federal government to reduce its role in the economy. Basically, westerners wanted free enterprise rather than government intervention:

> [W]e take the position that freedom from constraints is what westerners, producers, consumers, politicians, etc. are really seeking. This freedom from constraint could go as far as complete independence for western provinces, the last step to be sure, but which might be necessary failing all others. In a word, it is the philosophy of a return to economic liberalism which is the main thrust of this paper, and it is this which implies an end to economic exploitation as we see it. (Blackman 1981, 3).

Of course, in economics the term "economic liberalism" means free enterprise.

One of the most important issues for the future of the West, Blackman argued, was economic diversification. Much of the West's economy was based on non-renewable resources, such as oil and natural gas. Once these resources were gone there wouldn't be anything to replace them. So while revenues were coming in from the non-renewable resources, it was important for the western provinces to develop new industries that could replace the declining resources.

One would think that the federal government would have understood this issue and been in favour of the necessary diversification. But as Blackman argued, the reality of federal policy was otherwise:

> So it is that the process of industrial diversification in the west appears to be blocked at every turn. There is, firstly, the tariff policies which transfer income to eastern manufacturing regions from primary producing regions; secondly, a transport system which is so designed that prairie regions find it impossible to develop manufacturing because of the high commercial transport rates over the long distances to markets; thirdly, the statutory rates which discriminate against secondary food-processing industries; and fourthly, a feed grain assistance program and formula pricing for feed grains which discriminates against western livestock producers in favour of their eastern counterparts. All of these are so designed as to restructure comparative advantage against the western provinces so that instead of profiting from the specialization of production which confederation should make possible, western provinces are acting simply as sources of primary products for further processing in other regions of Canada.

> Finally, the National Energy Program itself discriminates against energy production within the provinces because of the low prices and consequent reduced netbacks to provincial producers. Further to this is the uncertain economic climate within which the energy industry itself must operate and which makes it all but impossible for small producers in particular to remain in the country. At the same time the Program, designed as it is to extract from the provinces as much low-cost energy resources as possible, reduces the future potential of a viable western petrochemical industry (Blackman 1981, 31).

The policies of the federal government were working directly against the interests of western economic diversification. And without that diversification, the western provinces would slip backwards into relative poverty, once the non-renewable resources were depleted.

In 1981, the NEP was the least popular of all federal policies in Alberta. It was a tool for exploiting Alberta. Beyond that, it was an effort to expand the size and power of the Canadian government. It was a socialistic policy:

> A federal bureaucracy will grow but never shrink. So it is that the people of Canada and confederation itself will eventually exist for the government and not the government for the people. The ultimate end of this tendency is government ownership and control of the means of production. The National Energy Program, of course, is precisely that, an economic plan for the ownership and production and sale of a resource via Petro-Canada. In doing so, the government provides for the capital funding, the skills, the marketing of the product, etc. on the "philosophical basis" that energy resources are just too important to be left to the private sector, but actually so that it may acquire the funds from the public to finance itself. The logical extension, of course, is the federal government's ownership of and production from **all** the basic resource industries until the point is reached, such as in Great Britain, that it becomes impossible to do without the government in the economic system. At that point we become saddled with an enormous burden of high cost, inefficiency, and a non-productive bureaucracy (Blackman 1981, 33).

Thus, an expansion of socialism within Canada was a direct result of the NEP.

But Blackman did not fail to emphasize the specifically anti-Alberta aspects of the NEP. For as he put it, "Marc Lalonde's statement at the beginning of the Energy Program, viz. 'It (the Program) must establish a petroleum pricing and revenue-sharing regime that recognizes the requirement of fairness to all Canadians no matter where they live' really means lower than market prices to consuming provinces. It is as simple as that. This we can refer to as deliberate exploitation" (Blackman 1981, 33).

He also addressed the widespread misconception that all or most Albertans were getting personally wealthy due to the high price of oil. As oil prices climb increasingly higher, most of it "is not made available to Albertans in the form of increased personal income. Contrary to popular belief, Albertans are not enjoying large increases in living standards due to 'high' prices of oil at the expense of other provinces" (Blackman 1981, 35). The fact that Albertans wanted market-based prices for their oil was not sinister. Blackman said that "it must be understood at the outset that an insistence on the world price for oil does not mean that Albertans are 'greedy,' 'selfish,' or Canadian 'oil sheiks.' Alberta is not Saudi Arabia where the wealth is concentrated in the hands of a feudal monarchy" (Blackman 1981, 38).

In sum, the federal government, Blackman deduced, was the root cause of western alienation. Blackman concluded that "it is the constraints imposed by the federal government which impede the achievement of the west's full potential; thus, it is the failure to remove these constraints which is at the root of the problem" (Blackman 1981, 40).

CONCLUSION

In a figurative sense, the federal government went to war with Alberta in 1980. This was not really a surprise at the time. The federal election campaign early in the year revealed a Liberal animosity towards Alberta that was very unsettling. It was clear that if the Liberals won and Trudeau became prime minister once again, Alberta would be in trouble.

Once the election was over and Trudeau was firmly in power, a showdown was just a matter of time. There was going to be a crisis and it was expected to be nasty. Under these circumstances many Albertans began to ponder the option of separatism.

The expected showdown did not disappoint, and with the NEP, Trudeau's Liberals invaded Alberta's oil industry. The indignation felt by many Albertans led to frequent and large separatist meetings. They weren't about to roll over for Pierre Trudeau.

Still, the separatist groups lacked the high calibre leadership that would make their movement into a formidable presence in the province.

Eventually, however, one separatist organization became registered as a provincial political party. And for a brief moment it looked as though separatism would make a real mark on Alberta.

REFERENCES

Alberta Report. 1980a. "The Crisis election." January 4: 9-11.

Alberta Report. 1980b. "Trudeau sets a collision course." February 8: 10-12.

Alberta Report. 1980c. "Alberta's separatist movement." March 28: 11.

Alberta Report. 1980d. "Alarm among the Liberals." July 18: 4-5.

Alberta Report. 1980e. "Separatism is growing." October 3: 6.

Alberta Report. 1980f. "Separatism surges." October 24: 7.

Alberta Report. 1980g. "Economic civil war." October 31: 2-5.

Alberta Report. 1980h. "Industry in chaos." November 7: 2-3.

Alberta Report. 1980i. "Separatism: 5% - 8% - 19% - 23%" November 7: 12-13.

Alberta Report. 1980j. "Fire on the prairie." November 14: 12-13.

Alberta Report. 1980k. "The cry for a free West." November 28: 2-3.

Alberta Report. 1980l. "Breakaway rivals." November 28: 7-9.

Alberta Report. 1980m. "Hu & the new West." December 12: 7-8.

Alberta Report. 1980n. "A separatist setback." December 19: 7-8.

Alberta Report. 1981a. "Dr. Hu & the name game." January 23: 5-6.

Alberta Report. 1981b. "Alive and nasty." February 6: 6.

Alberta Report. 1981c. "Horner is hooted down." February 27: 6.

Alberta Report. 1981d. "The National stays western." March 6: 6.

Alberta Report. 1981e. "Constitution land grab." March 20: 3.

Alberta Report. 1981f. "West-Fed's Calgary rupture." March 27: 4.

Alberta Report. 1981g. "Woes of West-Fed." April 10: 6-7.

Alberta Report. 1981h. "Alienation up, West-Fed down." May 29: 6.

Alberta Report. 1981i. "Blackman's blast-off." August 21: 2-3.

Blackman, W. 1981. *The Economics of Alienation: An Analysis of the Economic Roots of Western Canada.* Calgary: West-Fed Association.

Byfield, Ted. 1980a. "The election to tell if Canada is a confederation or an empire." *Alberta Report.* January 4: 44.

Byfield, Ted. 1980b. "The West must examine the price of being Canadian." *Alberta Report*. February 29: 44.

Byfield, Ted. 1980c. "What does Canada mean? It depends where you live." *Alberta Report*. March 28: 52.

Byfield, Ted. 1980d. "The case of the country that has vanished away." *Alberta Report*. April 11: 44.

Byfield, Ted. 1980e. "The budget: a political payoff venting an unbridled hatred." *Alberta Report*. November 7: 60.

Byfield, Ted. 1980f. "Old Canada or New Canada? You can't believe in both." *Alberta Report*. November 21: 52.

Byfield, Ted. 1981a. "The lull before the fury begins, a time to decide what if…" *Alberta Report*. January 16: 44.

Byfield, Ted. 1981b. "And now: Trial by bureaucrat, another Trudeau human right." *Alberta Report*. March 13: 52.

Byfield, Ted. 1981c. "A pariah of all the parties has a compelling proposition." *Alberta Report*. April 17: 52.

Byfield, Ted. 1981d. "So things would return to normal, eh, Mr. Lalonde?" *Alberta Report*. May 29: 52.

Byfield, Ted. 1986. "Farewell to the cowboy-economist." *Alberta Report*. September 8: 49-51.

Day, Stockwell. 1981. "The National: two views." *Alberta Report*. May 15: 19.

Harries, Hu. 1984. "Proof that Ottawa milks Alberta dry." *Alberta Report*. November 19: 23.

Harrington, Denise. 1981. "Who are the Separatists?" In *Western Separatism: The Myths, Realities & Dangers*, eds. Larry Pratt and Garth Stevenson. Edmonton: Hurtig Publishers Ltd.

Hopkins, Stephen. 1981. "The Alberta Blow." *Alberta Report*. March 13: 2-6.

Lewis, Robert. 1980. "Lougheed draws his wagons into a circle." *Maclean's*. November 10: 29-30.

Roberts, Stanley. 1980. "Separatism could mushroom." *Alberta Report*. February 29: 10.

Zwarun, Suzanne. 1980. "Separatism West: fact or fad?" *Maclean's*. December 1: 27-32.

CHAPTER 4

THE WESTERN CANADA CONCEPT PARTY: THE APEX OF ALBERTA SEPARATISM

THE WINTER OF 1980-81 HAD SEEN AN UNPRECEDENTED FLURRY OF separatist activity in Alberta. Many large meetings were held across the province. For the first time, Albertans were seriously considering the independence of their province as a means to defend themselves from the federal government of Pierre Trudeau.

By the late spring of 1981, much of the excitement appeared to have dissipated. Meetings were fewer and smaller. But during this period of relative calm, a new provincial political party had been registered, the Western Canada Concept Party of Alberta (WCC). And when a by-election was held to fill the seat of a retiring Social Credit MLA, the new party won. The election of Alberta's first separatist MLA shook the nation.

Despite the bright prospects for the WCC, however, it was unable to live up to expectations. It grew rapidly in the wake of its by-election victory, but growth also brought people of conflicting perspectives together. Division arose between soft-core and hard-core separatists. Supporters of rival leadership aspirants could not get along at times. The WCC earned a well-deserved reputation for internal squabbles, and this was a major factor in the party's inability to elect any MLAs in the 1982 provincial election.

With the wipe-out of the WCC in that general election, the glory days of Alberta separatism were over.

THE RISE OF THE WESTERN CANADA CONCEPT PARTY IN ALBERTA

In June 1981, Alberta Social Credit Leader Bob Clark resigned after being the MLA for Olds-Didsbury for 20 years. This meant there would be a by-election. Two days after his announcement, the WCC was officially registered as Alberta's first separatist party. It could therefore field a candidate in the by-election.

The WCC organizer for central Alberta by this time was Howard Thompson, brother of Robert Thompson, the former leader of the federal Social Credit Party. Howard Thompson believed the WCC candidate would do well in the by-election because many Albertans thought that Premier Lougheed wasn't doing enough to protect the province from Ottawa (*Alberta Report* 1981a, 2).

Thompson toured central Alberta in July with WCC founder Doug Christie. By the end of the month, the WCC reportedly had 21 constituency associations organized in Alberta, and about 2500 members. However, attendance at the meetings where Christie spoke was disappointing, with only 85 showing up at Olds, an important town in the by-election riding. Some people blamed Christie's behaviour for the low attendance. For example, *Calgary Herald* political writer Geoff White wrote about the WCC meeting in Bashaw and:

...slammed Mr. Christie for displaying "barely concealed scorn, even contempt" toward the small audience. According to Mr. White, obvious supporters were upset and alienated by the WCC leader. Following the meeting Mr. Christie was quoted with the explanation that it "is difficult to answer questions that are foolish questions" (*Alberta Report* 1981b, 5).

The general feeling was that people were not impressed with Christie.

Christie's leadership of the WCC in Alberta was soon questioned. The major reason for this appeared to be Christie's idea of how an independent western Canada would be governed. He wanted a unitary state for the West, to avoid the burden of a double layer of government that is involved in federalism. Federalism requires a federal and provincial government, so Christie wanted to abolish the provinces to eliminate one layer. But the emerging leadership of the Alberta WCC wanted to preserve existing provinces, notably Alberta.

The Alberta party became divided between the Christie loyalists and those who wanted to maintain Alberta as a distinct entity. Christie's faction was made up of a relatively small minority of party members. At a contentious September meeting, Edmonton realtor Allan Maygard was elected as the interim leader of the Alberta WCC and Hilton "Wes" Westmore was elected as the interim party president. This was, in effect, the end of Christie's role in the Alberta WCC:

> [T]he gloves really came off on September 12 at the Edmonton Inn, with 101 party members present. The Alberta executive was established with only nine dissenting votes, Mr. Westmore says, although Mr. Christie spoke against it three times. "Then he stomped out of the meeting when the vote went against him" (Sweet 1981, 10).

Christie then sent a letter to the Alberta WCC membership saying he would resign unless a meeting was held reaffirming his leadership. But no such meeting was held. This opened the door to cooperation between the Alberta WCC and what remained of West-Fed. The president of West-Fed, Stanley Cox, said, "I am predicting that we will be together in the near future as the major stumbling block, Mr. Christie, has been removed" (*Alberta Report* 1981c, 8).

The Alberta WCC held its first convention at the end of November 1981. About 300 members attended the convention, which adopted a party constitution, selected party officers and developed policy positions. The keynote speaker was University of Calgary economist Warren Blackman. At this point the party had a membership of about 3000 and 42 of the province's 79 constituencies had local WCC organizations. The official position of the party on separatism was hard-core. Party president Wes Westmore was quoted as saying, "We're going for an independent Alberta and we're not backing down. Then we hope the other western provinces would join us" (Byfield, V., 1981, 12).

In the fall, Marc Lalonde spoke in Sherbrooke, Quebec, about the "threat" of Alberta nationalism and how the federal government had to stand up to Alberta lest it become wealthy enough to impose its will on the other provinces. Ted Byfield pointed out that this was an admission of the true reason behind the NEP: "Its purpose is to show the West the tooth and claw of the central Canadian power base, and to smack Alberta down" (Byfield, T., 1981, 60).

One of the federal government tools for restraining Alberta was Petro-Canada, the oil company owned by Ottawa. It had bought out some other major oil companies as a means of increasing "Canadian" (read: federal government) control over the country's oil industry. It was an important government tool. Byfield referred to this company as Lalonde's "puppet pirate of the oil patch, Petro-Canada, which some call 'Toadycorp'" (Byfield, T., 1981, 60).

Petro-Canada had recently pulled out of an oil industry organization, the Independent Petroleum Association of Canada (IPAC), because IPAC opposed the Liberals' energy policy:

> Hence the industry is given an inescapable message from Toadycorp: If you want our business, support our government. Every participant in the industry with the "wrong" message is thereby forewarned and intimidated. The tooth and the claw are in action. We are being thrashed into submission (Byfield, T., 1981, 60).

The Alberta WCC continued to organize throughout the province, although mostly in rural areas. It was building on the decreasing popularity of Premier Lougheed, who was seen as not doing enough to protect Alberta. One WCC official stated, "Whether they admit it or not, the Tories have sold Alberta down the river" (Byfield, L., 1982a, 8).

On September 1, Lougheed had signed an oil agreement with Prime Minister Trudeau which many Albertans saw as a sellout. He and Trudeau then had a picture taken of themselves toasting the agreement, looking like friends. The WCC would use that picture in their advertising. Lougheed later regretted the picture. As he put it, "In political terms it was a dumb thing for me to toast the signing of the agreement with Mr. Trudeau and have my picture taken drinking champagne with him. I should have thought through the implications of the photograph" (Wood 1985, 181).

The WCC was holding meetings to build the party throughout the winter of 1981-1982. Leader Allan Maygard said, "In January we'll hold about 25 meetings throughout the province, about the same as most months. We'll get two or three hundred out to most meetings, and that's not small; what other party can say as much?" (Byfield, L., 1982a, 8). Maygard himself was a hard-line separatist, and he viewed the party as such as well: "A vote for us is a vote for separation from Canada; make no mistake about that" (Byfield, L., 1982a, 8).

The by-election for Olds-Didsbury was called for February 17. The Alberta WCC selected its deputy leader, Gordon Kesler, as its candidate. He was an oil scout and son of one-time champion cowboy Reg Kesler. His campaign slogan was "Send Ottawa a message" (*Alberta Report* 1982a, 6-7).

To the media and many political observers, the WCC had no chance of winning. A little over two weeks before the by-election, the *Calgary Herald* carried an article saying that separatist groups had "lost their steam." The article quoted Edmonton publisher Mel Hurtig as saying, "There is more need of an organization to combat warble flies than separatists in Alberta" (*Alberta Report* 1982b, 10). The media apparently did not accept the possibility a WCC victory in the by-election.

The provincial Tories chose lawyer Stephen Stiles to be their candidate. This was interesting because Stiles had been a West-Fed member and there was speculation that the PC Party had favoured him in order to neutralize support for separatism (Byfield & Byfield 1982, 8). It was a strategy that didn't work.

A couple of weeks before the by-election, Ted Byfield wrote that a WCC victory was "a very unlikely eventuality." However, should it occur it would cause a political earthquake: "The election of a separatist candidate in the only Alberta by-election held since Mr. Trudeau decided to get tough with us would shake the nation" (Byfield, T., 1982a, 52). He pointed out that a WCC win would have a number of benefits for Alberta because "Nothing seals the West's servitude more surely than the interminable reassurances of the Toronto-owned media that separatism here is dead" (Byfield, T., 1982a, 52).

On February 17, Gordon Kesler and the Alberta WCC received over 42% of the vote, whereas the Social Credit candidate received 28% and the PC candidate about 25%. *Alberta Report* described this result as:

> ...the biggest upset of Alberta politics since Tory Peter Lougheed swept the Social Credit from power 10 ½ years ago. The WCC victory made newspaper and television news across the nation and fundamentally changed the shape and conditions of politics in Alberta.... [T]he effect was to gain instant credibility for western separatism (Byfield & Byfield 1982, 6).

Upon winning the by-election Kesler stated, "I would hope Pierre Trudeau would wake up and read the results and, if we're lucky, he'll have a heart attack" (Legge 1982, 21).

Trudeau was very unhappy with the result, which he explained as follows:

> They've been spewing a great deal of hate against Ottawa and I think anyone, whether it's a federal or provincial election, knows that you do use a lot of – oh, what's that ugly word – racism against the French people in Ottawa, and what they're doing to this country, and also a lot of hate literature about how we're all Communists and we're going to try to

take their property away (*Alberta Report* 1982b, 11)

Alberta Report carried extensive coverage of the WCC by-election victory, written by Ted Byfield and his son Link. In a passage containing remarkable foresight based on historical knowledge, they stated the following:

> For the fledgling WCC, of course, the by-election could mark either the beginning or the end. If Alberta politics follows the pattern they took in 1966 when a by-election in Pincher Creek landed, of all things, an NDP member in the legislature, it could bode ill. The then Premier E. C. Manning stumped the province in a general election five months later warning of a threatening socialist apocalypse. He swept the province and that was the end of the NDP seat in Pincher Creek. If Premier Lougheed can so use the threat of a separatist holocaust in Alberta, he too might wipe out the gain in a quick succeeding general election (Byfield and Byfield 1982, 9).

Interestingly, WCC leader Allan Maygard was hoping that Lougheed would wait a whole year before calling a general election. The WCC needed time to organize and to introduce itself to Albertans. In the by-election aftermath party members were exhilarated, and there were even rumors that some backbench Tory MLAs were considering switching to the WCC (Byfield, V., 1982a, 8).

A poll taken by *Alberta Report* at this time placed WCC support at about 14% across the province. This result was reported on CBC-TV in Edmonton:

> Then the CBC posed a similar query as its "Question of the Day": "If a provincial election were called tomorrow, how would you vote?" The switchboard was promptly swamped with 1,800 calls – one of the highest responses ever to this frequent CBC feature. Of these, 827 were for the WCC, 420 for the PCs, 324 NDP, 156 Liberal, 68 Socred and five undecided (Byfield, V., 1982b, 11).

During March, Alberta West-Fed president Bob Matheson held a press conference to announce that his organization would now officially support the WCC. Previously West-Fed and the WCC had been seen as rivals, so this development was positive for the separatist cause in Alberta (Byfield, V., 1982c, 8).

GORDON KESLER
IN THE ALBERTA LEGISLATURE

Gordon Kesler was the first separatist MLA in the Alberta Legislature and he actively participated in some legislative debates. Occasionally, his comments or questions reflected a separatist stance. On March 22, 1982, he had an exchange with Premier Lougheed. He asked:

> If Alberta cannot get a better deal for the oil industry, if Alberta cannot gain control of its agricultural industry, if Alberta cannot stop compulsory metrification, if Alberta cannot bring about a stop to compulsory bilingualism, and if Albertans' rights of freedom and heritage are going to be stripped away by the federal policies, will the Premier of Alberta take Alberta out of Confederation, in order to preserve the greatness of this province and the dignity of its people?

Lougheed replied:

> Mr. Speaker, the answer is, clearly and unequivocally, no. But within the ambits of some of the matters raised by the hon. Member for Olds-Didsbury, there is no doubt that the province will continue, as it has in the past – and with considerable success in the past – to assure that the rights and interests of the citizens of Alberta, as Canadians, are fully respected (*Alberta Hansard* 1982, 244).

A few days later there was discussion in the Legislature about Canada's new constitution being approved by the British Parliament. One opposition MLA asked the government what kind of celebrations would be planned to mark that event. Kesler jumped into the discussion asking, "In some of those programs anticipated for bringing home the constitution, have you considered flying the Alberta flag at half-mast?" (*Alberta Hansard* 1982, 341). His question was ignored.

In April, the new constitution came up again. This time there was a government motion for the Legislature to give formal assent to the new constitution, proclaimed by the Queen on April 17, 1982. In speaking against the motion Kesler said, "I think April 17 will go down in history as one of the saddest days we've ever experienced in this country" (*Alberta Hansard* 1982, 653).

Kesler's main concern about the new constitution was its failure to entrench property rights. He went on at length about this issue in the Legislature more than once. At one point he basically proposed that Alberta should separate from Canada if property rights were not enshrined in the constitution:

> Let us have a statement that Albertans can have property rights in their constitution. Let us take the issue to Albertans in a referendum, and ask them: if property rights cannot be put into the constitution of Canada, are you in favor of creating a new state where Albertans' property rights can be guaranteed in the constitution? (*Alberta Hansard* 1982, 654).

Later that same day, Social Credit MLA Walter Buck asked Kesler himself some questions about a constitution for an independent Alberta. He asked, "If the hon. Member for Olds-Didsbury is to lead Alberta out of Confederation, can he indicate to the Assembly under which constitution Alberta would be operating?" Kesler replied:

> The province of Alberta will be operating under the constitution that the people of this province will put together. That will be decided at conventions of Western Canada Concept, and there will be input from the people of this province on what they want in a constitution.

Buck followed that answer with another question: "Would the hon. member indicate to the Assembly and the people of Alberta if he would be leading Alberta out of Confederation in consultation with other members of the western provinces, or just Alberta?" Kesler responded:

> Mr. Speaker, the answer is that we would certainly work very closely with the other provinces of western

Canada. We would be in consultation with them, so
that finalization would be in accordance with plans so
that they could be brought in as a unit (*Alberta Hansard*
1982, 655).

As it turned out, Kesler would be an MLA for only a few months.

PARTY INFIGHTING AND
THE PROVINCIAL ELECTION OF 1982

Toward the end of March, the Alberta PC Party held its annual meeting in Edmonton. By this time, it was widely recognized that the WCC
posed a major threat to the PCs. With that threat in mind, delegates
to the meeting passed a resolution calling for the Alberta government
to renegotiate the September 1981 energy agreement that Premier
Lougheed had made with Prime Minister Trudeau. In his speech to
the gathering, Lougheed said that the September agreement moved
the federal forces "from the living room to the porch." But he signaled
a tougher line by then adding, "I'm beginning to think we ought to
move them off the property" (Byfield, V., 1982d, 8).

The WCC continued to grow rapidly throughout the spring. The Alberta Social Credit Party was collapsing, and some of that party's members and activists were joining the WCC. Even one of the MLAs who
had been repeatedly elected under the Social Credit banner, Ray Speaker, was considering joining the WCC. Alberta Liberal leader Nick Taylor, a long-time observer of Alberta politics, declared "unequivocally
that an immediate election here would be won outright by the WCC"
(Byfield, V., 1982e, 7).

With rapid growth and successful meetings being held at various points
in the province, the WCC had 69 of the 79 provincial constituencies
organized by April 22. More critical attention was being focused on the
party since it had not yet issued a complete policy statement. People
began to wonder what the party really stood for. As well, differences
among party figures over the issue of separation began to emerge. The
leader, Allan Maygard, and the president, Wes Westmore, were hard-
line separatists who definitely wanted Alberta to become independent
of Canada. But other major figures, such as MLA Gordon Kesler and

72

Edmonton Zone Director Dr. Fred Marshall, were soft-liners because they viewed the threat of separation as a way to get a better deal for Alberta within Canada (Byfield, V., 1982f, 7).

On April 15, Maygard issued a formal statement saying that "Western Canada Concept Party advocates Independence for Western Canada." It then went on to say the party favoured such positions as one official language, protection of property rights, the use of referendums, and a few other policy positions. It closed by saying, "When Western Canada Concept forms the government we will proceed with the necessary steps to prepare for independence in a peaceful and democratic manner." This statement had been ratified by the party's board of directors (Maygard 1982, 6).

In early May, however, it looked like the Alberta WCC could break apart. At a 17-hour meeting, the board split into two warring factions: the Maygard-led hard-liners and the Kesler-led soft-liners. The soft-liners won. Maygard, Westmore and two other board members resigned. Kesler was made interim leader in Maygard's place. He expressed regret over the conflict but said the party would be better off without its radical element (Byfield, V., 1982g, 6-7).

The WCC planned a policy convention for July 15-17 in Red Deer, and as the date approached, party infighting continued. Elmer Knutson's membership in the party was officially cancelled by the board, and it was expected that Maygard's and Westmore's memberships would also be cancelled. Don Braid of the *Edmonton Journal* predicted that the party might self-destruct at the convention, and Maygard "charged that the WCC is now controlled by a clique of Mormon directors, led by devout Mormon Kesler" (Byfield, V., 1982h, 8).

The July convention, however, went very well. Organized by Howard Thompson, the proceedings went rather smoothly and "the party emerged more united than ever before" (Byfield, V., 1982i, 6). There were 420 voting delegates and another 200 or so other members present. Voting was held to elect a new party president (Harold Schultz of Calgary), first vice-president (Dr. Fred Marshall of Edmonton) and second vice-president (Al Oeming of the famous game farm near Edmonton), as well as other board members. On a motion initiated by

Stockwell Day of Edson, Elmer Knutson's and Doug Christie's memberships in the party were reinstated. Economist Warren Blackman gave the banquet speech in which he called for unity between the hard-line and soft-line wings of the party (Byfield, V., 1982i, 10).

In a column published shortly afterwards, Ted Byfield pointed to the significance of the WCC's Red Deer convention:

> It was extraordinary for what it implied. Who could have imagined, say, 24 months ago that such a diverse throng could be assembled in the province of Alberta to declare that, under given conditions, they are ready to break up the country. It was extraordinary also in another way. The rank and file were far more impressive than the leadership. Here was no strident rabble or convocation of kooks. You met doctors, grain growers, lawyers, accountants, cattlemen, housewives, scientists, small businessmen, teachers, executives (Byfield, T., 1982b, 44).

Clearly, the party could no longer be construed as just a small group of wackos. Respectable people were involved in a significant way. Trudeau's anti-Alberta policies had led to a notable change in Alberta's political scene.

Besides becoming more united, the WCC scheduled a leadership convention for August 21. Six men vied to lead the party. The most significant were Gordon Kesler, Howard Thompson, Elmer Knutson and Jack Ramsay. Ted Byfield wrote at the time that the "current leadership campaign of the Western Canada Concept could be of profound significance not only to Alberta but to the whole country" (Byfield, T., 1982c, 52). Byfield said that the West had three options: the status quo, independence, or a better federal system for Canada where the weaker resource-producing provinces are protected. Few people in Alberta favoured the status quo, and only a minority favoured independence. Most people favoured an improved Canada. But how could Canada be improved?:

> How then could such a change be brought about? Only, replies the WCC, if there exists in the West a

74

political movement with its priorities absolutely clear. First choice, a Canada with a truly federal system of government. Second choice, an independent West. Utterly unacceptable, the status quo, the system that brought the Trudeau-Lalonde scourge upon us. In other words, we will only get a real country if we are prepared to go it alone. Reluctantly prepared, but prepared nevertheless. That is a very compelling answer (Byfield, T., 1982c, 52).

Indeed, that was the soft separatist position: separation if necessary, but not necessarily separation.

Gordon Kesler won the WCC's leadership contest at the convention in Red Deer on August 21. On the first ballot he received 250 votes, Howard Thompson received 186, and the other four candidates received a combined total of 96. Three of these four then endorsed Thompson, but on the second ballot Kesler won with 284 votes to Thompson's 246. Except for Elmer Knutson, the defeated candidates pledged their support for Kesler. The convention went very well for the party. Reporters "searched their memories in vain as they tried to recall a leadership campaign and convention, of any party, conducted with such almost unnatural gentlemanliness. The WCC was determined to live down its reputation for dirty fighting" (Byfield, V., 1982j, 7).

Unfortunately, the gentlemanliness did not go much deeper than outward appearances. Howard Thompson's supporters – who were very numerous – expected Kesler to reach out to Thompson to offer him a high profile position within the party, such as deputy leader. But Kesler did nothing of the sort. Thompson and a number of his supporters thus left the party, and in the provincial election Premier Lougheed called for November 2, Thompson and a number of his people backed a coalition of independent candidates called the Provincial Rights Association (PRA). Basically, a key component of the WCC had split off, severely weakening the party. Kesler's people blamed Thompson and said he was a "sore loser" (Byfield, V., 1982k, 6-8).

In the midst of the election campaign, Ted Byfield pointed out the benefits of electing some WCC candidates to the legislature. For one thing, if some WCC-type MLAs had been elected in the previous provincial election, Alberta wouldn't have ended up in such a bad position. "Surely it is obvious that if something like the WCC had been holding 10 or 20 seats in the Alberta legislature in the year 1980, the National Energy Program simply could not have happened" (Byfield 1982d, 60).

Byfield did not recommend electing the WCC to be Alberta's government. But he did believe it would be best if some WCC candidates were elected. He said, "what we could and might do is send a half dozen of them into the opposition. There, their presence would represent a solemn warning to the Trudeaus, Lalondes and other vultures that there is a distinct limit to what they can do to the West. And they have definitely reached it" (Byfield, T., 1982d, 60).

The election campaign did not go well for the WCC. Only 15 candidates had been nominated at the time the election was called on October 5, and the Thompson people had just left the party. Kesler had difficulties dealing with the media. And then there was "the characteristically turbulent departure from the WCC of West-fed founder Elmer Knutson, charging that Mr. Kesler had forbidden him to stand as a candidate" (Byfield, L., 1982b, 8):

> WCC party organization had meantime continued chaotic, producing curious situations like the one in which leader Kesler lashed out at *Alberta Report* as a Tory mouthpiece, while some dozen individual constituencies sought – and received – permission to reprint and distribute the publisher's letter from the magazine's October 11 issue. The burden of this editorial message added to the joke. The WCC's leader might be lacking, wrote publisher Byfield, but the party's basic principles were sound and were desperately needed (Byfield, V., 1982l, 11).

In the election of November 2, the WCC did not win a single seat. Kesler had run in the Highwood riding where he lived rather than the Olds-Didsbury riding he had represented as an MLA. In Highwood he received 18% of the vote while the PC candidate received over 70% of the vote. It was a wipe-out for him. Overall, the WCC had a province-wide 11.8% of the vote compared to the PCs' 62%. The NDP won almost 19%, far better than the WCC. Some individual WCC candidates did relatively well, coming in second to the PC candidate. The WCC candidate in the Ponoka riding received over 33% of the vote and the candidate in the Wainwright riding received 29% of the vote, for example. But the shut-out was a major disaster for the party.

When the media approached Kesler for his response to the defeat, he delivered a "graceless harangue" in which he chided voters who he said had "seen fit to elect a Socialist government." He said the PCs had bought the voters with their own money, and that the media had "slandered" and "assassinated" him and the party (Byfield, V., 1982l, 10). He was obviously bitter.

Some party members saw Kesler himself as the problem. Edmonton Avonmore's 1982 WCC candidate, Pastor Jake Johnson of the Bible Baptist Church, told me in an interview that "Kesler was a disaster for the Western Canada Concept." In his view Howard Thompson would have been better.

Economist Ralph Hedlin attributed the election outcome to Premier Lougheed's "pro-Canadian heroics." But he also had a warning:

> The people of Alberta and their leader have proffered their hand in friendship to all their fellow-Canadians. The vote in Alberta was premised on a confidence in the dedication and determination of Peter Lougheed and, as anyone who toured the constituencies through the recent campaign can confirm, it definitely was not approval of the exploiters and centralists who have worked so long to centre decision-making in Ottawa, Southern Ontario and the St. Lawrence Valley. If it is interpreted as a statement of Alberta subservience it will be a disaster for Canada. The match is withheld from the fuse for a further four years. There is now time to rearrange confederation. If central Canadians make a folly of the promise he gave, not even Lougheed will be capable of staying the subsequent deluge (Hedlin 1982, 20).

The immediate separatist threat posed by the WCC had been thwarted. But that did not mean that Albertans had embraced the existing situation. Indeed, the potential for separatism was still very real.

CONCLUSION

West-Fed and the WCC were able to hold well-attended meetings during the winter of 1980-81 due to Albertans' anger at Trudeau, Lalonde and the NEP. By the spring and summer of 1981, however, it looked like the excitement was over. But in this case, appearances were very deceiving.

In June, the WCC was able to register as an Alberta provincial political party. Coincidentally, a long-time Social Credit MLA resigned, necessitating a by-election to fill his seat. That by-election was called for February, 1982. No one in the media appeared to see what was coming. The WCC's victory in that by-election set off a second wave of separatist excitement. It looked like the new party would play a significant role in Alberta's future.

But once again appearances were deceiving. The WCC was its own worst enemy. Frequent infighting was usually the result of struggles between soft-core and hard-core separatists, or between the supporters of rival leadership figures. Whatever the case, the WCC scuttled its own promising future. Premier Lougheed's early election call and skillful handling of the situation, undoubtedly also contributed to the WCC's demise in the 1982 general election.

The WCC needed credible and capable leadership to achieve electoral success. But leadership just wasn't there in a form that could take the party to the next level. Instead, the WCC got infighting, internal dissension and defeat.

The party would try to pick itself up after the November 1982 debacle. At points it looked like it could even make a comeback. Interest in separatism was on the rise again in Alberta by 1986-87. But the final opportunity for an Alberta WCC comeback was thwarted by the rise of another new western-rights party, the Reform Party of Canada.

REFERENCES

Alberta Hansard. 1982.

Alberta Report. 1981a. "Separatist resurgence." July 3: 2.

Alberta Report. 1981b. "Struggling separatists." July 31: 5.

Alberta Report. 1981c. "The uniting separatists." October 23: 8-9.

Alberta Report. 1982a. "Intriguing by-election possibilities." February 8: 6-7.

Alberta Report. 1982b. "A problem of credibility." March 1: 10-11.

Byfield, Link. 1982a. "From anti-Trudeau to anti-Lougheed." *Alberta Report.* January 25: 8.

Byfield, Link. 1982b. "High noon in Highwood (and all's not well)." *Alberta Report.* November 1: 8.

Byfield, Link, and Ted Byfield. 1982. "The rebellion in Olds-Didsbury." *Alberta Report.* March 1: 6-11.

Byfield, Ted. 1981. "Mr. Lalonde brags in Quebec of how he stopped Alberta." *Alberta Report.* November 6: 60.

Byfield, Ted. 1982a. "The terrible but plausible threat in Olds-Didsbury." *Alberta Report.* February 8: 52.

Byfield, Ted. 1982b. "What the WCC does, matters; why it exists matters more." *Alberta Report.* July 26: 44.

Byfield, Ted. 1982c. "The West has three options and we'll soon have to choose." *Alberta Report.* August 9: 52.

Byfield, Ted. 1982d. "Only the separatists, you say? Pity . . ." *Alberta Report.* October 25: 60.

Byfield, Virginia. 1981. "Separatist politics: hot to trot." *Alberta Report.* December 11: 12-13.

Byfield, Virginia. 1982a. "The by-election aftermath." *Alberta Report.* March 8: 6-8.

Byfield, Virginia. 1982b. "The separatist legislator claims his seat." *Alberta Report.* March 15: 11.

Byfield, Virginia. 1982c. "Swallowing their pride." *Alberta Report.* March 22: 8-9.

Byfield, Virginia. 1982d. "Now for the Tory counter-attack." *Alberta Report.* April 5: 6-8.

Byfield, Virginia. 1982e. "The chaos in the opposition." *Alberta Report.* April 19: 6-7.

Byfield, Virginia. 1982f. "The nagging separatist dilemma." *Alberta Report.* May 3: 6-7.

Byfield, Virginia. 1982g. "Bar the doors – cut off the phones." *Alberta Report.* May 17: 6-7.

Byfield, Virginia. 1982h. "Feuding racks the separatist camps." *Alberta Report.* July

12: 8.

Byfield, Virginia. 1982i. "Renaissance at Red Deer." *Alberta Report.* July 26: 6-10.

Byfield, Virginia. 1982j. "Kesler: the winner by 38 votes." *Alberta Report.* August 30: 6-8.

Byfield, Virginia. 1982k. "The fracturing of the right." *Alberta Report.* October 25: 6-8.

Byfield, Virginia. 1982l. "The WCC looks for someone to blame." *Alberta Report.* November 15: 10-12.

Hedlin, Ralph. 1982. "Peter's pro-Canadian heroics left the fuse unlit – for now."*Alberta Report.* November 15: 20.

Legge, Gordon. 1982. "A shout of western protest." *Maclean's.* March 1: 21.

Sweet, Douglas. 1981. "Separation plagues the separatists." *Alberta Report.* October 2: 10.

Maygard, Al. 1982. "Statement of Independence." *Alberta Report.* May 3: 6.

Wood, David G. 1985. *The Lougheed Legacy.* Toronto: Key Porter Books Limited.

CHAPTER 5

THE PARTIAL RECOVERY OF THE ALBERTA SEPARATIST MOVEMENT

Dedicated members of the WCC tried to pick up the pieces after the November 1982 election debacle. In a February 1985 by-election, the party had a respectable showing despite not winning the seat. The WCC then spent a fruitless year trying to form an alliance with Alberta's numerous small, right-wing parties. This effort prevented the WCC from being prepared for the May 1986 provincial election, and it barely registered when the votes were counted.

But as 1986 progressed, Albertans' disappointment with the Mulroney government turned to anger for its failure to remove the Trudeau government's Petroleum and Gas Revenue Tax (PGRT), and its decision to give the CF-18 maintenance contract to Montreal instead of Winnipeg. This helped fuel support for separatism, but it also led to the creation of the Reform Party of Canada. The Reform Party would then quickly absorb the support of those who had been angered by Mulroney, letting the air out of the separatist balloon.

SEPARATISM AFTER THE NOVEMBER 1982 ELECTION

Hard-line separatists immediately blamed Kesler's soft-line on separatism for the WCC's election defeat. Doug Christie had a letter published in the *Calgary Herald* making this exact point. The election, he said:

> has proven the futility of soft soap and fudging. Kesler should resign and make way for a separatist to lead the WCC and build it with principles. Separatism is the heart of the party, and a party without heart is dead (Byfield, L., 1982, 8).

Wes Westmore, who had been ousted as Alberta WCC president earlier, began work to found a new Alberta separatist party. In his view, "Vacillating, soft pedaling, taking the middle of the road on the separatist issue has killed the WCC in Alberta" (Byfield, L., 1982, 8).

Kesler took a very different position. He argued that the party had actually done well, despite not winning any seats. As he put it, "We did pretty well in the election, considering our inexperience. It took us one year to get 12% of the vote, despite an exceptionally heavy Conservative turnout. It took the NDP 40 years to get that far" (Byfield, L., 1983a, 8).

Kesler also reiterated his view that independence was only a last resort. The official WCC position under his leadership was that the West should first strive to reform Confederation before making any moves towards separating from Canada. This was the position that angered the hard-core separatists.

By the spring of 1983, Ted Byfield was publicly lamenting the failure of the Alberta WCC to take any seats in the election. The actions of both the federal Liberal and federal PC parties continued to favour central Canada at the expense of the West. Writing in May he said:

> The scripting of political and economic events in this country in the last three months looks as though it

82

was written by the late, lamentable Western Canada Concept party. Certainly everything that has happened precisely fulfills the most dire predictions of that much deplored group. And it is safe to say that most of it would not have happened if a few of them had been elected last year to the Alberta legislature (Byfield, T., 1983, 52).

Byfield was referring to two events in particular. The federal transport minister had proposed replacing the Crowsnest Pass freight rate, which subsidized grain transport, with a direct subsidy payment to farmers. His proposal would have helped the meat industry on the prairies to flourish at the expense of the meat industry in Toronto and Montreal. The Quebec Liberal caucus killed the plan.

Secondly, the federal PC Party was having a leadership campaign, and none of the three leading contenders, Joe Clark, Brian Mulroney, and John Crosbie, would commit to allowing Alberta to receive better than 75% of the world price for oil.

Byfield feared that the 1982 election had sent the wrong message to central Canada. The failure to elect any WCC candidates gave the Trudeau Liberals the impression that:

> the West is thoroughly and unequivocally Canadian, true blue right to the end. Kick'em. Walk on 'em. It doesn't matter. The West loves it. Look what happened in Alberta. Big fuss about separatism there. But the separatists never elected a single member. This means Ottawa can do anything it likes to the West any time it feels like it (Byfield, T., 1983, 52).

Shortly after Byfield's editorial was printed, Kesler appeared publicly on the front steps of the Alberta legislature to present the WCC's manifesto for the province's economic recovery. He was no longer a separatist, and favoured removing the party's independence plank from its constitution. He also thought the party should try to forge a conservative coalition with the two independent MLAs who had formerly been with the Social Credit Party, Ray Speaker and Walter Buck (Byfield, L., 1983b, 9).

Most party members were not happy with Kesler and his non-separatist position. When the party held a general membership meeting on June 25, 1983, 170 members attended. The hostility to Kesler was so obvious that he opened the meeting by resigning. When a vote was held on the independence issue, 64% voted to keep separatism as official party policy. As a result, 5 non-separatist board members resigned (Lee 1983, 9).

This posed a bit of a dilemma for Wes Westmore. He had already been working on setting up the Alberta Independence Party (AIP). Despite the clear separatist orientation of the Alberta WCC, Westmore believed that the AIP would provide the separatist movement with a fresh start (Lee 1983, 9).

With Kesler gone, the party decided to reach out to 20 people whose party memberships had been revoked during the provincial election campaign. Most of those 20, including former leadership contender Howard Thompson, rejoined. At this point, party membership was estimated to be about 2000, down from a high of 12,000 during the election campaign (McCarthy 1983, 7).

But the conflict over the party's commitment to separatism continued unabated. At its annual convention in Edmonton in November 1983, a motion to remove independence from the list of party goals was narrowly defeated. Interim president and acting leader Fred Marshall himself wanted to downplay the separatist image. However, by the end of the convention a compromise motion passed by a wide margin, weakening, but not entirely removing, independence from the party's goals (Fennell 1983, 7).

Early in April 1984, the Alberta and Saskatchewan provincial WCC parties announced plans to organize a federal WCC party. Led by Hugh Clark of Saskatchewan, the new party planned to run the required 50 candidates in the upcoming federal election (Byfield, L., 1984, 9). These plans did not come to fruition, and there were no WCC party candidates in the federal election.

However, Elmer Knutson's recently organized Confederation of Regions Party (COR) did successfully qualify for official status for the election. COR managed to find 54 candidates in the four western provinces, including 20 of Alberta's 21 ridings. All 14 of Saskatchewan's ridings had COR candidates as did 10 of Manitoba's 14 and 10 of BC's 28. One of the Alberta candidates was former Edmonton alderman Robert Matheson, who had previously held prominent positions in the Independent Alberta Association and West-Fed. Getting COR registered for the election with 54 candidates was described as "Knutson's crowning achievement" (Dabbs 1984a, 7).

The COR Party was not an explicitly separatist party, although Knutson's position could arguably be accused of being a form of soft-core separatism. But COR was an explicitly western-rights party; its purpose was to defend the West. In his penultimate pre-election editorial, Ted Byfield recommended voting for COR:

> Every vote cast for this new group will make things that much easier for the provincial government when it negotiates with Ottawa, or for the Alberta caucus in a Mulroney government. For a modest turn-out on behalf of COR – 20% of the total, say – would have to mean that the resource steal had done infinite damage, that outright separatism was far from dead, that international prices must be implemented immediately on western oil, that the demands for the Triple-E Senate had to be taken seriously, that the current plan to force compulsory bilingualism on a province without allowing the people to vote on it is ill-advised and must be scrapped, in short that Ontario and Quebec have pushed the resource provinces as far as they can safely push them. All of which, of course, would vastly ease the job of anyone negotiating with Ottawa, whether a backbench Alberta MP, or a provincial cabinet minister. For this reason if I were living in any Alberta constituency where the Liberal vote in the last election was not formidable, then I would vote for COR, and I would do all in my power to persuade my neighbours to do the same. That way, somebody down there will hear us (Byfield, T., 1984a, 44).

COR was a brand new party at the federal level and not very well-known. Not surprisingly, therefore, none of its candidates were elected. It received about 2.2% of the vote in Alberta, less in BC and Saskatchewan. However, it did receive 6.7% of the vote in Manitoba, due to controversy over compulsory bilingualism in that province. Brian Mulroney's PCs received a whopping majority of parliamentary seats (211 to the Liberals' 40, and NDP's 30), including all seats in Alberta and most seats in Quebec.

THE POLITICAL THOUGHT
OF ELMER KNUTSON

Elmer Knutson was the founder of West-Fed in 1980 and of the Confederation of Regions (COR) Party of Alberta, and a federal COR party in 1984. He always resented the label of being a separatist, which was confusing to many people since West-Fed was considered to be a leading separatist organization.

The reason he could lead an organization widely believed to be separatist, while denying that he was a separatist, was because he had a very peculiar view of Canadian constitutional law and history. He did not believe that Canada's federal government had been legally constituted and therefore it did not have legitimate authority. Each of the provinces, in his view, was technically independent already. He could not be a separatist if there was no central political entity to separate from.

In 1983, Knutson self-published a book-length defence of his views, together with some historical documentation he believed provided evidence for them. The book was called *A Confederation or Western Independence?*

Knutson summarizes his basic theory as follows:

> We did not Federate in 1867, and the Governor-General was a corporation sole until the Statute of Westminster was enacted. What are we now? We certainly are not a confederation, as there has been no confederation since that date. The authority was given to the provinces. They were made equal with Great Britain. The power went to the provinces. Ottawa was never a province or a colony. How did it get authority? It was only a

committee of men, half appointed and half elected, to aid and advise the Governor-General…. The provinces are Sovereign and will remain so until we the people, through our Provincial Governments, create a country (Knutson 1983, 78).

In 1931, the British Parliament passed the Statue of Westminster which recognized a more equal relationship between Britain and the former British colonies that had become Dominions, like Canada. Canada's status as a country independent of the British government was more clearly recognized than ever before. This statute was a key component in Knutson's theory:

Upon the passage of the Statute of Westminster, all provinces (or former colonies) became sovereign, self-governing and independent, and by Eminent Domain have a future right to stay independent, Federate or form a union and none were or are superior to the others (Knutson 1983, 80).

The main proponent of these views before Knutson was a Social Credit Member of Parliament from Alberta, Walter Kuhl. Kuhl gave a long speech in the House of Commons in 1945 outlining this argument. Years later he retired to Spruce Grove. Knutson wrote that Kuhl "and I have spent many hours discussing true Canadian history. It is fair to say that I have learned much from him" (Knutson 1983, 91). No doubt about that.

Knutson was also very concerned about the growth of government and the threat that growth posed to individual freedom. Government had become a "gigantic burden" on the economy, and "this massive and mindless government intrusion has almost destroyed the most precious of our worldly holdings – our personal freedom" (Knutson 1983, 102). In his view, all three of the major parties, Liberal, PC and NDP, accepted the expansion of government to one degree or another. Thus a new political party would be necessary to reverse the trend.

Knutson believed the four western provinces should form a Western Federation and the Atlantic provinces should form an Atlantic federation. With Quebec and Ontario remaining as they are, Canada would then have four formal regional groups. Together they could form a Confederation of Regions (hence the party name). The regions would control their own local matters and the confederal government would presumably handle matters such as foreign affairs and defence.

If the Confederation of Regions idea was not going to work, however, Knutson believed the West should assert its independence. Knutson proposed to "establish a true Western Conservative Right Wing Party, which is not affiliated with or controlled by Ontario." This party could "become the next government of Alberta, and the catalyst for a Western Federation which can and will break the political power structure of Canada – or failing that, independence at some future date so we can be masters of our own house" (Knutson 1983, 116). Western independence was definitely the fall-back position.

Knutson was very concerned about the power exercised by Ontario and Quebec over all of Canada. The situation would remain like this until the political structure of the country was changed:

> The Central Canadian government in Ottawa is continuing to impose powers akin to those of a master over a slave upon the people of Western Canada. Westerners do not have enough votes to protect their rights and resources against any Ottawa regime with support in Ontario/Quebec (Knutson 1983, 123).

The Confederation of Regions proposal would solve the problem. But Knutson always seemed to add that independence was the only other option, and one he would support if the confederation idea failed. He closed his book as follows:

> Yes, I personally am prepared after a Western Federation is formed to give one last try to reconstruct and unite Canada. But the truth is, I do not hold out much hope. The strength will only come if Ontario perceives us as being serious. I am serious, I want a quick Solution, I want equality or Independence and Self Determination. That is my right. It is the legacy our forefathers handed us; we must not fail our future generations. Our Duty to them is clear (Knutson 1983, 128).

Knutson was a Western patriot, and he put his money where his mouth was. There may even have been some merit in his Confederation of Regions idea. But the view that the provinces were sovereign entities was a misreading of constitutional history. Few people seem to have taken it seriously.

SEPARATIST DEVELOPMENTS IN THE MID-1980s

In his final editorial before the 1984 federal election, Ted Byfield reflected on Quebec's success in achieving its goals within Confederation. He pointed out that the man who had done the most for Quebec was René Lévesque. Quebec had elected Lévesque and his party, threatening to take the province out of Confederation. With this pressing threat, the federal Liberal government worked hard to keep Quebec happy. Byfield recommended that Alberta do the same:

> At the provincial level we need a party that is committed to fundamental constitutional change, aimed at liberating us from the dominance of the centre, a party that says we want to be partners in a confederation, not subjects of a central Canadian empire. We want into Canada or we want out. You cannot keep us on the basis you have us now (Byfield, T., 1984b, 52).

In other words, Byfield wanted Alberta to have a provincial party willing to threaten separation in order to get a fair deal for the province within Canada.

Interestingly, it was right at that time that the Alberta WCC was having its leadership convention. There were two candidates: Dr. Fred Marshall of Edmonton who wanted to play down the separatist issue, and Jack Ramsay of Camrose who argued "that independence must be preserved as a solid threat if any worthwhile concessions are to be wrung from central Canada" (Dabbs 1984b, 7).

The Alberta WCC was using the best technology of the time for its leadership convention on August 25, 1984. The candidates would be at a central location in Red Deer and their speeches were broadcast by satellite TV to 18 locations around the province for members to watch.

89

Then the party members could vote by phone and the results would be broadcast on TV from the Red Deer location (Dabbs 1984b, 8).

Ramsay, the stronger pro-separatist, won easily with 418 votes to Marshall's 174 votes. Clearly, the Alberta WCC was still a separatist party (Dabbs and Weatherbe 1984, 8). However, Marshall was elected party president at its subsequent convention in Red Deer in November. By that point the membership numbered about 1500 (Dean and Weatherbe 1984, 7).

In October 1984, the Alberta provincial NDP leader, MLA Grant Notley, was killed in a plane crash. A by-election was subsequently called for February 21, 1985, to fill his seat for the Spirit River-Fairview riding. Notley had held that rural northern seat since 1971, although each of his election victories had been by small margins.

Seven parties ran candidates in this by-election: the PCs, NDP, and Liberals, of course, as well as four small right-wing parties, WCC, COR, Social Credit and the tiny Heritage Party. The WCC candidate was a popular local farmer, Daniel Fletcher.

In the run-up to the by-election, Ted Byfield implicitly endorsed the WCC. He pointed out that the new Mulroney government had not abolished the Petroleum and Gas Revenue Tax (PGRT), which taxed the oil industry on its revenues instead of its profits. It had been instituted by Trudeau, and Mulroney seemed suspiciously uninterested in abolishing it. The PGRT (also known as Please Get Rid of Trudeauism) was an onerous burden on Alberta's key industry. But Byfield knew how to get rid of this tax:

> It is in the power of some Albertans, a very few, to kill the PGRT. Its removal could, in fact, be decided very soon, not in Ottawa, but in our own north country. If in the forthcoming by-election in Spirit River, the Tories or the Liberals or the NDP win, then the PGRT will probably stay. If the Western Canada Concept wins, and the whole country becomes alarmed about attitudes in the West, then the PGRT will suddenly vanish away. That is the lesson Quebec has taught us, and if we fail to learn it, we deserve what we get (Byfield, T., 1984c, 44).

The NDP won the by-election in a reasonably tight 3-way race between that party, the PCs and the WCC. The WCC came a strong third with 25% of the vote. The other right-wing parties were well behind the WCC. These smaller parties were seen as pulling votes from the WCC which otherwise would have performed even better. Ted Byfield wrote that Elmer Knutson should now throw the provincial wing of his COR party behind the WCC to strengthen the cause of western constitutional demands.

Byfield drew a number of conclusions about Alberta politics from this by-election. One was that the future of the Alberta WCC was bright:

> Most significant of all in the result was the strength shown by the WCC. It was the only group in the by-election to demonstrate increased support since 1982 and the increase was enormous. Between the general election and the by-election the NDP vote fell by 27%, the Tory vote went down by 37%. The WCC rose by 56%, thereby establishing the movement (for anyone who does not embrace socialism) as the alternative party in Alberta. Moreover, it is now well entrenched in the third-place position that has proved so consequential in Alberta politics (Byfield, T., 1985a, 52).

However, the leadership of the WCC drew a different message from the by-election. Besides their party, there were three other small right-wing parties that split the vote on the right: Social Credit, COR, and the Heritage Party. If these parties' votes had been combined, it would have put them in a close second in the by-election. Why split the right-wing vote?

The day after the by-election, WCC executives met with Alberta Social Credit leader Martin Hattersley to discuss a merger of the parties. Over the summer the two parties worked out an agreement to merge as the Alberta Political Alliance (APA). This meant that the WCC was dead as a separatist option. APA spokesman Hugh Duxbury stated, "Separatism is stupid and unnecessary, and the Socreds and the new party will have nothing to do with it" (Elash 1985a, 6). The basis of union was a 10-point statement of principles that emphasized free enterprise and the economic interests of Alberta.

At the November 1985 convention of the Alberta WCC, 90% of the 85 delegates voted in favour of folding the party into the APA. A by-election was scheduled for an Edmonton riding in December as a way to get the new Alberta PC leader and premier, Don Getty, a seat in the legislature. The APA ran its first candidate in that by-election, former Social Credit cabinet minister Lucien Maynard (Elash 1985b, 6-7). However, Maynard only received about 3.5% of the vote, an extremely poor showing.

Early in April 1986, the Alberta WCC decided to pull out of the APA. The APA had not yet written a party constitution, scheduled a founding convention, or begun working on a plan to prepare candidates for the impending provincial election. An election was expected soon, and the WCC, claiming a membership of 10,000, planned to run 20 candidates (Campbell and Orr 1986, 9-10). In short, immediately after the Spirit River-Fairview by-election, the Alberta WCC had gone on a year-long rabbit trail with the APA.

Another notable event occurred after that by-election: Ted Byfield began pushing hard for the Triple E Senate. Undoubtedly, his columns on this issue were a significant contribution to popularizing the Triple E Senate idea. It was offered as a specific alternative to separatism. Byfield mentioned that certain policies work against the western interest, because politicians want the votes of people in Ontario. He then added, "It is this indisputable fact that has driven some westerners to the dire extreme of separatism. The more rational alternative is the Triple-E" (Byfield 1985b, 52).

Another column supporting the Triple-E Senate in April 1986, floated the interesting idea of creating a new western federal political party to replace the federal Tories. Mulroney's government had been dragging its feet on eliminating the NEP, and even when much of that program was dismantled, the Petroleum and Gas Revenue Tax (PGRT) was only to be fazed out over a period of time, disappearing finally in January 1988. It was beginning to look like Alberta wasn't going to receive justice from any of the three conventional parties. If that was the case, "We would need a Party of the West, which can sell its support to the highest bidder in exchange for the Triple-E. If the Mulroney Tories fail us, then that is the way we must go" (Byfield 1986a, 52).

A general election was called for Alberta for May 8, 1986. The WCC was only able to muster 20 candidates, and the provincial wing of COR six candidates. As well, hard-core separatists ran three candidates as independents:

> Calgary engineer Hilton (Wes) Westmore was a co-founder of the WCC who left the party after it dropped separatism from its platform and is now managing the crusade of Okotoks farm girl Pamela McIver, 19, in the Highwood riding. The other contenders are William Deacon from Banff-Cochrane and Tom Erhart in Mountain View. The aim of the admittedly hastily arranged and ill-organized campaign is to keep the separatist option alive and before the electorate (Orr 1986, 9).

The vote results for both the WCC and COR were very bad, partly at least due to running such a small number of candidates. The WCC got 0.65% of the provincial vote total, a far cry from 1982. And COR received 0.40% of the total vote. Some individual candidates weren't complete write-offs. The Ponoka-Rimbey WCC candidate received over 12% of the votes in his riding, and the Wainwright WCC candidate received close to 8% in his . The 19-year-old independent separatist candidate received 7.9% of the votes in her riding. And Elmer Knutson came second in Olds-Didsbury, receiving 23% of the votes there. But, of course, none of these candidates even came close to winning.

Although people like Wes Westmore viewed the WCC as having abandoned separatism altogether, that wasn't quite true. Certainly the WCC took a soft separatist position at this time, but it hadn't abandoned separatism completely. In a letter-to-the-editor of *Alberta Report* in July 1986, Alberta WCC leader Jack Ramsay freely held out the separatist option. He wrote that "Alberta will never have long-term economic stability until we have equality within confederation (e.g. a Triple E senate) or independence" (Ramsay 1986, 3). So independence was certainly still a possibility if other efforts failed, in the view of the Alberta WCC.

During 1986, Alberta was experiencing a recession, largely as a result of low oil prices. By August, respectable oilmen as well as some Alberta politicians, including MP Jack Shields, were speaking out against the continued existence of the PGRT. But there was no political party for these disaffected people to turn to for support, according to Ted Byfield. He wrote that "The old Western Canada Concept party seems dead, and lacks credibility" (Byfield 1986c, 14). Two weeks prior to that, after outlining problems with the federal government, he had asked, "Is our case therefore hopeless? I don't think so. What we need is a credible western party" (Byfield 1986b, 52).

By this time, Byfield had lost interest in separatism and was arguing in favour of a new western federal party, which of course, would later emerge as the Reform Party of Canada. Towards the end of August 1986, he wrote:

> Surely, what we need to develop quickly but astutely is a western Canadian party. Separatist, you say? The old Western Canada Concept dragged out of its unpropitious past? Not separatist at all, the very opposite of separatist, in fact, because instead of seeking to destroy the country, it would seek to make it work (Byfield 1986d, 52).

Early in 1986, the Tory MP for the Alberta riding of Pembina had resigned to run in the provincial election. In August, a by-election was called for September 29. BC separatist and WCC founder Doug Christie decided to run in the by-election as an independent candidate, because the WCC didn't have a registered federal wing. Elmer Knutson ran as the COR Party candidate. Separatist sentiment had, in fact, been increasing during the summer of 1986, largely due to federal indifference to Alberta's economic problems.

Alberta Report's first article about the coming by-election was entitled, "Separatist resurgence." It was expected that the by-election would give some indication of the strength of disaffection with the Mulroney Tories in Alberta. Premier Don Getty even mentioned publicly that separatism was growing again in the province:

> Speaking to a luncheon crowd at the Canadian Bar Association convention in Edmonton last Wednesday, Alberta Premier Don Getty was angry: "I feel in Alberta

a frustration that we don't have the kind of policies coming out of Ottawa we hoped we would have. Once we thought it's because we're not supporting the Liberal government. But now we've supported the Conservative government, and there's still this sense of frustration." Later, Mr. Getty told reporters he's encountered a renewed spirit of separatism in Alberta. "I get it in my mail, my phone calls, and my travels" (Orr and Caldwell 1986, 6).

Early in the by-election campaign, the Tories were trailing in a riding that had been one of their strongholds. Likely due to the fear of losing the riding, the Mulroney government suddenly cancelled the PGRT, more than one year ahead of schedule. There were also increasing indications of a separatist revival in Alberta. A poll at the time "conducted by Winnipeg-based Angus Reid Research revealed that 23% of 304 Albertans polled think there will be majority support for separatism in the province within the next few years" (Campbell and Weatherbe 1986, 7). This poll, as well as Don Getty's experiences, provided evidence of the separatist surge.

In the 1984 federal election, the PC candidate won the Pembina riding by 34,000 votes. In the September 29, 1986 by-election, the PC candidate won by just 232 votes over the popular NDP candidate, former Edmonton mayor Ivor Dent. Many Albertans had become disillusioned with the Mulroney government after just two years. But most of them did not turn to separatism. As Ted Byfield explained,

> Why, then, did they not vote separatist? Well, as a matter of record, one in 11 of them did, even though one of the separatist candidates was widely viewed as both anti-semitic and dangerous. More probably, they did not vote separatist because they are not separatist. They think the Canadian system doesn't work, but they are not prepared to split the country over it. So they did not vote at all (Byfield 1986e, 52).

By this time, Doug Christie had been defending James Keegstra, an Alberta public school teacher accused of promoting a Jewish conspiracy theory to his students. Christie, Keegstra's lawyer, was seen as being more than a little sympathetic to Keegstra's views and was, therefore, considered by many to be anti-Semitic. This hurt the separatist cause, because Christie was widely identified with separatism. People who may otherwise have been predisposed towards separatism did not want to be seen as fraternizing with anti-Semites.

But the Mulroney government was becoming almost as unpopular as the Trudeau Liberal government had been in Alberta. James Coutts, a close Trudeau adviser from 1975 to 1984, publicly predicted that the federal PCs would lose all of their Alberta seats if an election were held. But he didn't think the Liberals or NDP would pick up the seats. Instead, he believed a new party would emerge to dominate the province. As he put it, "All that is missing is a prophetic leader who understands the depths of the grievances and will promise a vision of hope and bold action" (Jenish 1986, 15). Coutts would be proven right in 1993.

In November 1986, the Alberta WCC held its convention in Calgary with the theme of "Back to Separatism." Leader Jack Ramsay declared that the party would "return to its roots" of advocating independence for Alberta. He discerned a rising separatist tide, and critics within the party faulted him for waffling on separatism, so he was willing to adopt a stronger separatist stance. The party membership at the time was between 700 and 1000 (Slobodian and Cybulski 1986, 11).

Alberta WCC president Fred Marshall said that there were an increasing number of separatists in Alberta. He said that "the situation now has the potential for being the same as it was at the time of the Olds-Didsbury by-election, or even stronger" (Slobodian and Cybulski 1986, 12).

The Mulroney government gave separatism a huge boost at the end of October 1986. Companies from Winnipeg and Montreal had been competing for a federal contract to maintain the Canadian military's CF-18 fighter jets. According to the rules of the competition, the Winnipeg firm won the contest. But to please Quebec, Mulroney instead awarded the contract to the Montreal company. It was a case of pure political expediency; Quebec was more important than Manitoba.

The effect was immediate and powerful. According to *Alberta Report*, "an interest in separatist or radical pro-western movements broke out with fierce intensity" (Byfield et al 1986, 10). In fact, this article stated that "Not since October 28, 1980, six years ago almost to the day, had the cause of western separatism been given such a boost" (Byfield et al 1986, 10).

PETER BRIMELOW
AND ROBERT MANSELL

During the fall of 1986, two important studies appeared that bolstered the case of western separatism. One was a book by Peter Brimelow, who had been a business journalist in Canada during the 1970s. Originally from Britain, he had later moved from Canada to the United States and wrote his book as an outside observer. The second study was an economic analysis of fiscal transfers within Canada.

Peter Brimelow's book was called *The Patriot Game: Canada and the Canadian Question Revisited*. The book explained how the federal Liberal Party had managed to dominate Canadian politics in the latter part of the twentieth century, and had used federal government power to make significant changes to the country through such policies as bilingualism and multiculturalism. English Canada had been duped into allowing the Liberal Party to completely remake the country in a liberal-left mold.

Brimelow's main arguments were music to the ears of western separatists and other conservatives. He was able to powerfully articulate the discontent many English-speaking Canadians had with the direction their country had been taking since the 1960s. But in some places he also seemed very sympathetic to western separatism. Brimelow describes the NEP "as a classic case of aggression against the West by the Central Canadian establishment" (Brimelow 1986, 248). And he understood what was really behind the NEP:

> In the last analysis, the National Energy Program was really a National Political Program. By subjugating the burgeoning, politically deviant West, it served the needs of both the elected and permanent governments – where the two can be distinguished, not always easy

in Canada. To a remarkable degree, the NEP was the creation of an identifiable group of federal civil servants in the Department of Energy, Mines and Resources who were explicitly motivated by considerations of what they called "equity" – that is, a disapproval of Alberta and the oil companies getting rich and a determination to make them share the wealth with the federal government and its clients (Brimelow 1986, 249-250).

Brimelow provided a brief description of separatist elements in western Canada and he was optimistic about the future of western separatism. As he put it, "in 1981, the various separatist groups did of course poll better in Alberta than similar groups in the Quebec provincial election of 1966. If precedents hold, all it needs is a leader – and about another ten years" (Brimelow 1986, 255).

Interestingly, in a different place in the book he seems to predict the coming rise of the Reform Party of Canada. He said it was clear that *"sectional divisions within English Canada will be a continuing problem. This is particularly true of the Western provinces. They may lead some sort of rebellion against the Liberal hegemony, perhaps by supporting a right-wing, fourth party"* (Brimelow 1986, 288).

There is much in this book that is valuable from an Alberta separatist standpoint, but one last tidbit will do. Brimelow quotes from an early 1983 *New York Times* article about the Socialist International. It noted that although the Liberal Party of Canada was not a member of that organization, Pierre Trudeau had close ties with some of its leaders. Speaking of Trudeau, the article says, "One official of the New Democratic Party said there were 'obviously key people in his Cabinet who we know are socialists though we'd never admit that publicly'" (Brimelow 1986, 48). So what many Albertans feared – that Trudeau's government was strongly influenced by socialists – was likely true.

The Patriot Game received considerable media attention when it appeared, much of it negative. But *Alberta Report* did a cover story on the book that included many excerpts. Naturally, the story was wholly positive (Slobodian and Whyte 1986, 56-60).

Around the time that Brimelow's book came out, University of Calgary economics professor Robert Mansell released a report showing that Alberta had sent about $90 billion net dollars to Ottawa since 1969. He produced his report in response to anti-Alberta press accounts that had appeared in central Canada.

> Prof. Mansell arrived at his total by combining two figures. First, he balanced all federal revenues raised in a province against all federal expenditures. Here he discovered Alberta's net loss between 1969 and 1984 to be $30 billion. (The net Ontario outflow over the same years was less than $6 billion.) Second, he determined that the regulated, artificially low domestic price of oil since the early 1970s has cost Alberta another $60 billion (Cybulski et al 1986, 9).

What did Mansell conclude from this? As he put it, "The story told by these numbers is overwhelming. They're draining Alberta to pump up central Canada" (Cybulski et al 1986, 9).

Mansell was not a separatist. He believed Canada could work if changes were made, such as the adoption of a Triple E Senate. He believed something was necessary to prevent Ottawa from pillaging Alberta for the benefit of central Canada. For as he saw it, "The reason the federal government rode roughshod over the Alberta government's resource rights was to show Quebec and to a lesser extent Ontario, that there was good reason to stay in confederation" (Cybulski et al 1986, 11).

Mansell would continue his work along this line and in 1992, a significant study co-authored with Ronald Schlenker was published. Reviewing the figures for federal fiscal balances during the period 1961-1989, the authors wrote, "federal policies have had very significant impacts in terms of the regional distribution of GDP, population, and employment. In particular, they have reduced the size of Alberta in terms of GDP, population, and employment compared to what it would otherwise be" (Mansell and Schlenker 1992, 234).

It is not unreasonable to suggest that when one province is excessively wealthy, such as Alberta during the oil boom, it should share some of its wealth with the poorer provinces. But the corollary would be that once the excessive wealth dissipates, the extraction of wealth for the benefit of others should cease. Unfortunately, when the oil boom collapsed and Alberta fell into recession in the mid-1980s, the federal government continued to gouge the province, making the province's grave economic situation even worse. Mansell and Schlenker state "that it was the federal policies that produced the extremely large net outflows that were mainly responsible for the very deep and prolonged recession in Alberta" (Mansell and Schlenker 1992, 237).

During the recession of the mid-1980s, the Alberta government of Premier Don Getty initiated policies to help the province's economy, but these efforts were undermined by the federal government; "the continuing large federal fiscal surplus with Alberta served to neutralize the fiscal deficits which the provincial government was running in an attempt to stimulate the Alberta economy" (Mansell and Schlenker 1992, 237). The federal government helped to prevent an economic recovery in Alberta.

But it wasn't just with this one incident that the federal government undermined Alberta. The province has historically had a boom-and-bust kind of economy because it is based on natural resources. Sometimes resource prices are up, sometimes they're down. The economy is up or down, following the price trends. So it is somewhat unstable. But the federal government has made this instability even worse: "on balance over the past three decades federal policies taken as a whole have been more a source of economic instability in the case of Alberta than a source of stability" (Mansell and Schlenker 1992, 238).

Mansell and Schlenker were not separatists at all. But after looking over the economic evidence they said, "It is fairly clear that, considering only the fiscal impacts, an independent Alberta would have a significantly larger economy" (Mansell and Schlenker 1992, 251). And they concluded, in part, as follows:

> For most of the historical period the net contributions by residents of Alberta have been many times larger than one would expect given their relative income levels and any reasonable definition of equity. This result has also been observed in other analyses of fiscal

balances. Over this period at least, the term "milch cow of Confederation" is more appropriately applied to Alberta than it is to Ontario or any other region (Mansell and Schlenker 1992, 260).

Alberta was, according to the best economic analysis, getting shafted.

SEPARATIST GROWTH IN 1987

In the aftermath of the CF-18 decision, support for a Triple E Senate was increasing in Alberta. A senate that had equal representation from each province, was elected rather than appointed, and would be effective (that is, have real powers), was being advocated not only by Ted Byfield, but also by Alberta Premier Don Getty and other prominent citizens. But Alberta WCC leader Jack Ramsay saw the quest for such a senate as hopeless. As he put it, "The hope for equality within confederation through a Triple E Senate is a futile but necessary phase through which we must pass before Albertans accept independence as our only alternative" (Ramsay 1987, 4).

In June, 1987, six Calgary businessmen began an attempt to form the Alberta Separatist Party (ASP). They were former members of the Alberta WCC who felt their former party was too soft on separatism. If the ASP were elected as the Alberta government, it would immediately begin negotiations with the federal government to pull Alberta out of Canada. The ASP spokesman, William Harman, predicted it would get 15% of the vote in the next provincial election and win 10 to 15 seats in the legislature. Jack Ramsay dismissed the new group saying "Bill Harman and his bunch failed to win the leadership in the WCC, so now they're splintering the separatist vote by forming their own party and appointing themselves to lead it" (Koch 1987a, 10). Apparently the ASP never got off the ground.

A few months later, in October, 1987, a federal separatist party, the Western Independence Party (WIP), was formed at a meeting of 50 people in Edmonton. Dr. Fred Marshall was chosen as interim leader. One purpose of forming this party was to have a separatist organization completely unconnected to Doug Christie, who was increasingly seen as anti-Semitic. As Marshall stated, "we've already divested ourselves of the racist image by breaking with Christie" (Koch 1987b, 15).

101

In September, PC MLA Henry Kroeger passed away. Shortly thereafter a by-election for his rural riding of Chinook was called for November 23. Jack Ramsay ran as the Alberta WCC candidate. The PCs won the by-election with almost 52% of the vote, but Ramsay came second with over 21%. At least in some parts of rural Alberta, the WCC was the PCs' main rival. It certainly appeared that the WCC was starting to make a comeback.

Strangely, however, that would be the very last election contested by the Alberta WCC. In May 1988, the party name was officially changed to The Alberta Independence Party (AIP). Eleven months later, in April 1989, it was officially deregistered as a party for failure to file the required financial statements with Elections Alberta.

In an informal phone conversation I had with Dr. Fred Marshall towards the end of 1989 (if memory serves me correctly), he told me that separatist activists had decided to work within the Reform Party of Canada. The Reform Party had done well in Alberta in the federal election of November 1988. As well, it had won a by-election in March 1989, and therefore had an Alberta MP in Ottawa. For citizens concerned about defending Alberta, the Reform Party was clearly the way to go. Nothing succeeds like success. Indeed, Alberta WCC leader Jack Ramsay became a Reform Party MP in the 1993 federal election. The pro-Alberta elements that would have sustained an Alberta separatist movement were subsumed within the new Reform Party of Canada.

CONCLUSION

During the period of separatist resurgence, from 1982 to 1987, something else was also going on: Preston Manning, Ted Byfield, and others began work on the creation of a new western party. The Reform Party of Canada had the credible leadership that separatist groups had been unable to develop, and it had the backing of prominent citizens. Its quick success in attracting support, and then in electing an Alberta MP in March, 1989, caused people who otherwise would have supported separatism to see it as the best alternative for Alberta. Separatism in Alberta evaporated – temporarily.

REFERENCES

Brimelow, Peter, 1986. *The Patriot Game: Canada and the Canadian Question Revisited.* Toronto: Key Porter Books.

Byfield, Link. 1982. "Forging a new and true separatist party." *Alberta Report.* December 6: 8.

Byfield, Link. 1983a. "And now a race for the WCC." *Alberta Report.* February 21: 8.

Byfield, Link. 1983b. "Kesler returns to cry 'sell-out'." *Alberta Report.* June 13: 9.

Byfield, Link. 1984. "The prairie WCC goes federal." *Alberta Report.* April 16: 9.

Byfield, Ted. 1983. "Two prize examples of how the system works against us." *Alberta Report.* May 16: 52.

Byfield, Ted. 1984a. "The best result for Alberta: 16 Tories, 4 COR & one Liberal." *Alberta Report.* August 27: 44.

Byfield, Ted. 1984b. "How to make Mulroney's win a western victory." *Alberta Report.* September 3: 52.

Byfield, Ted. 1984c. "Mulroney's missing Rule 11 has a message for Spirit River." *Alberta Report.* December 31: 44.

Byfield, Ted. 1985a. "The NDP won, but the real Tory nemesis is the WCC." *Alberta Report.* March 4: 52.

Byfield, Ted. 1985b. "It's now or never for Triple-E reform." *Alberta Report.* March 11: 52.

Byfield, Ted. 1986a. "We will soon know whether what Trudeau told us is true." *Alberta Report.* April 21: 52.

Byfield, Ted. 1986b. "Whoever runs, it doesn't matter: Ottawa still writes us off." *Alberta Report.* August 4: 52.

Byfield, Ted. 1986c. "Oil's ominous protest." *Alberta Report.* August 18: 12, 14.

Byfield, Ted. 1986d. "Masse makes it inescapable: the West needs its own party." *Alberta Report.* August 25: 52.

Byfield, Ted. 1986e. "The 17,665 non-voters who tell the real story of Pembina." *Alberta Report.* October 13: 52.

Byfield, Ted, D'Arcy Jenish, Mary Nemeth, and Jonathan Cote. "The CF-18 rip-off." *Alberta Report.* November 17: 10-19.

Campbell, Donald, and Fay Orr. 1986. "Parties part." *Alberta Report.* April 14: 9-10.

Campbell, Donald, and Stephen Weatherbe. 1986. "The Tories nose ahead." *Alberta Report.* September 22: 6-7.

Cybulski, Henry, Stephen Weatherbe, Tim Gallagher, Rudy Haugeneder, Paul Bunner, and D'Arcy Jenish. 1986. "The milking of Alberta." *Alberta Report.* October 6: 9-12.

Dabbs, Frank. 1984a. "The stubborn rise of COR." *Alberta Report.* August 20: 7-8.

Dabbs, Frank. 1984b. "Separatism or just a bluff?" *Alberta Report*. August 27: 7-8.

Dabbs, Frank, and Stephen Weatherbe. 1984. "Separatism if necessary." *Alberta Report*. September 10: 8.

Dean, Philippa, and Stephen Weatherbe. 1984. "The WCC tries populism." *Alberta Report*. December 3: 7.

Elash, Anita. 1985a. "Striving for a right-wing resurrection." *Alberta Report*. November 4: 6.

Elash, Anita. 1985b. "Unity on the fringe." *Alberta Report*. December 2: 6-7.

Fennell, Tom. 1983. "Alberta's feuding WCC reunites." *Alberta Report*. November 21:6-7.

Jenish, D'Arcy. 1986. "Coutts calls for cataclysm." *Alberta Report*. October 27: 14-15.

Koch, George. 1987a. "More prairie protest." *Alberta Report*. July 6: 10.

Koch, George. 1987b. "A crowded fringe." *Alberta Report*. November 2: 14-15.

Knutson, Elmer. 1983. *A Confederation or Western Independence?* Edmonton: E. Knutson.

Lee, Robert. 1983. "WCC: sick but still separatist." *Alberta Report*. July 4: 9.

Mansell, Robert L. and Ronald C. Schlenker. 1992. "A Regional Analysis of Fiscal Balances under Existing and Alternative Constitutional Arrangements." In *Alberta and the Economics of Constitutional Change*, ed. Paul Boothe. Edmonton: Western Centre for Economic Research, 211-281.

McCarthy, Shawn. 1983. "Shuffles among the separatists." *Alberta Report*. September 5: 7-8.

Orr, Fay. 1986. "Alberta readies to dig out the vote." *Alberta Report*. May 5: 7, 9.

Orr, Fay, and Linda Caldwell. 1986. "Separatist resurgence." *Alberta Report*. September 1: 6.

Ramsay, Jack. 1986. "We still need the Triple E." *Alberta Report*. July 21: 3.

Ramsay, Jack. 1987. "Separatism follows a Senate cry." *Alberta Report*. May 11: 4.

Slobodian, Linda, and Henry Cybulski. 1986. "Back to separatism in Alberta." *Alberta Report*. October 27: 11-12.

Slobodian, Linda and Kenneth Whyte. 1986. "Brimelow and the big picture." *Alberta Report*. November 10: 56, 58, -60.

CHAPTER 6

THE REFORM PARTY DISAPPEARS AND ALBERTA SEPARATISM REAPPEARS

B Y THE LATTER HALF OF 1986 AND INTO 1987, SEPARATISM WAS surging again in Alberta. This was especially the case after the Mulroney government gave the CF-18 contract to a firm in Montreal, in October 1986.

But that surge was intercepted by a new phenomenon, the formation of the Reform Party of Canada. For those concerned about Alberta's rights within Canada, the Reform Party had at least two big advantages over separatism: its remedy was relatively moderate and therefore had much larger potential appeal, and it had the credible leadership that the separatist movement had failed to acquire.

With those advantages, as well as some early successes under its belt (a by-election victory and a senate election win in Alberta), the Reform Party quickly became the unrivaled vehicle for pro-Alberta sentiment. Separatism faded away.

However, in 2000, the Reform Party dissolved and was replaced by the Canadian Alliance. When eastern Canadians spurned the Canadian Alliance in the federal election of November 2000, many patriotic Albertans felt they had nowhere to turn except to separatism. The Alberta Independence Party (AIP) looked like it was going to really take off, but its failure to formally register as a provincial party, and other difficulties, saw the party fade away by the end of 2001.

The Separation Party of Alberta officially formed in 2004, but has had little success. The victory of the Conservative Party of Canada in the January 2006 federal election has helped to dampen separatist sentiment in Alberta, because Stephen Harper became prime minister. He has a long track record defending Alberta's interests and is widely viewed as being a reliable westerner. Once he leaves, or perhaps if he compromises too far in pursuit of votes in Ontario and Quebec, separatism will likely grow in Alberta.

THE REFORM PARTY
ABSORBS ALBERTA SEPARATISTS

Throughout 1986, two key westerners began to call for the formation of a new federal political party for western Canada: Ted Byfield and Preston Manning. Byfield mentioned the need for a new party in some of his *Alberta Report* columns. Manning began having lunch and dinner appointments with business and political contacts to discuss the possibility of a new party. In September, he wrote and circulated a memo entitled "A Western Reform Movement: The Responsible Alternative to Western Separatism" (Dabbs 1997, 103).

In October, the Mulroney government gave Montreal the CF-18 contract and many people in western Canada were outraged. That provided an opportunity for Manning to build support for his idea of a new party and the Reform Association of Canada was formed. Its first meeting, the Western Assembly on Canada's Economic and Political Future, was held in Vancouver in May 1987. A large majority of the delegates at that meeting endorsed the idea of forming a new political party. At the end of October of that same year, over 300 voting delegates attended the founding convention of the Reform Party of Canada in Winnipeg, and selected Preston Manning as leader (Dabbs 1997, 122-131).

The Reform Party was not a separatist party by any means. The first party slogan was "The West Wants In." Nevertheless, the party would attract the support of at least some soft separatists. Frank Dabbs notes:

> The Vancouver and Winnipeg founding assemblies had been energized by an ill-defined anger at Ottawa stemming from the National Energy Program and CF-18 decision. The meetings drew support from strong federalists disenchanted with the old parties and also had the endorsement of soft separatists (Dabbs 1997, 147).

Certain people who had played key roles in the Alberta separatist movement quickly became Reform Party of Canada supporters. It has already been noted that Ted Byfield occasionally advocated a soft separatist position in his columns, and he was one of the most important early promoters of the Reform Party. As early as the preparation stage for the Vancouver assembly of May, 1987, "Howard Thompson, the former Socred and WCC organizer from Innisfail – helped recruit delegates from rural Alberta" (Manning 1992, 135). Thompson, of course, had also been a West-Fed organizer, and he came close to winning the leadership of the Alberta WCC in 1982. He went from the WCC to the Reform Party.

Former Edmonton alderman Bob Matheson had been a major figure in the Independent Alberta Association in the 1970s, and also with West-Fed in the early 1980s. Preston Manning notes that in the late 1980s, Matheson "had been active in organizing the Reform Party in Edmonton" (Manning 1992, 201). Matheson had tried to become the Reform Party's candidate for the 1989 Alberta senate election but lost to Stan Waters.

Jack Ramsay was the leader of the Alberta WCC from 1984 at least until 1988. As noted, he promoted Alberta separatism in that capacity. He joined the Reform Party and was one of its candidates in the November 1988 federal election. He won his seat for the Reform Party in the 1993 and 1997 federal elections – after being the leader of Alberta's separatist party for about four years.

Many more people who had been prominent in the Alberta separatist movement shifted to the Reform Party in the late 1980s. This was not accidental. Preston Manning wrote that "one of my initial motivations for promoting the Reform Party was to provide an effective and constructive alternative for westerners who were leaning toward the separatist option out of frustration" (Manning 1992, 167). The Reform Party was conceived, in part, as a way to bring separatists back into the federalist fold. And it worked.

Since important leadership figures in the Alberta separatist movement were early converts to the Reform Party, it is only reasonable to conclude that the rank-and-file of the movement also switched to the Reform Party. Judging from the virtual absence of separatist activity in Alberta during the lifetime of the Reform Party, it seems likely that Alberta separatists who didn't jump on the Reform Party bandwagon simply faded out of political activity.

The Reform Party did reasonably well in Alberta in the 1988 federal election, even though none of its candidates were elected. It received about 15% of the province-wide vote, and nine Reform Party candidates finished second. In March 1989, Deborah Grey won a by-election for the party with 51% of the vote, becoming the first Reform Party MP. In October of that year, Stan Waters won Alberta's senate election as the Reform Party candidate with 42% of the vote (Dabbs 1997, 136, 140, 142).

Clearly, the Reform Party was on a roll. It had been formed out of the same kind of regional discontent that had earlier fueled western separatism, and its leadership figures were reliable westerners. On the night she was elected, Deborah Grey stated her priorities as follows: "The first issue is for westerners to get a fair shake. This is the message to Ottawa" (Howse 1989, 12). Thus, any Albertan with separatist tendencies would view the Reform Party in a favourable light. It had become the political vehicle for pro-Alberta types for the duration of its existence.

Although the Reform Party decided to expand nationally in 1991, it was still largely seen as a western party. In the 1993 federal election, 52

Reform Party MPs were elected, mostly from Alberta and BC. Only one was from outside the West, in Ontario.

By the mid-1990s, some conservatives in Canada were expressing concern about vote-splitting between the Reform and PC parties. If these two parties were splitting Canada's right-wing vote, the Liberals would remain in control of the federal government indefinitely. Merging the two parties would put an end to Liberal dominance, it was argued.

Pro-western elements were not convinced. As Link Byfield put it, "The West's party is the Reform, and a merger with anyone will represent nothing except 10 years of wasted effort" (Byfield, L., 1997, 2). This was because "all 'merging' ever amounts to for westerners is submerging" (Byfield, L., 1997, 2). Reform was the West's party and it represented western interests in Ottawa. From a pro-Alberta perspective, it was still the political vehicle of choice.

In the federal election of early June 1997, the Reform Party won a few additional seats for a total of 60 and became the official opposition. It lost its one seat in Ontario and so was more western-oriented than before, at least in terms of its caucus. It continued to be seen as the West's party.

Ted Byfield figured there would be a showdown with Quebec in the wake of the 1997 election. In his view, the West had not been properly represented before at the constitutional bargaining table, but this time things would be different:

> Well, this time we will be represented, and by a unanimous voice at Ottawa: that of the Reform Party. This is extremely important. The whole inclination of Ottawa, whether Tory or Liberal, will be to sacrifice western interests in various ways as bribes to mollify Quebec. The Reformers are in a particularly good position to resist this fiercely. They needn't defer to their Ontario wing, or their Quebec wing, because they have none. They can unambiguously represent the West (Byfield, T., 1997, 44).

The Reform Party, ten years after its founding, could still "unambiguously" represent the West. There was no need for a separatist movement in Alberta to get Ottawa's attention.

But the splitting of the right-of-centre vote in Canada in the 1997 federal election added fuel to the case of those advocating some sort of party merger between Reform and the PCs. By early 1999, Preston Manning had embarked on an initiative called the United Alternative (UA) to bring together conservative-minded citizens into one federal party. Some individual Tories joined the effort, but the PC Party had no intention of becoming a part of it.

Although most Reform Party members would come to support the UA, many western members were concerned about its effects on the West. As *Alberta Report* noted, "Rank-and-file Reformers in the West distrust Ontario and sometimes detest their Tory rivals at the local level. Rightly or wrongly, they deeply fear that union with such compromised partners will place the party beyond the control of both the West and the existing party membership" (Gibson and Byfield 1999, 8). It went on to report that "some disenchanted Reformers have discussed a western separatist party if Mr. Manning is successful in lobbying for UA" (Gibson and Byfield 1999, 9). So once it appeared that Reform may be gone, talk of separatism immediately began.

Early in 2000, however, a majority of Reform Party members voted to fold the party into the Canadian Alliance, the result of the UA. The Reform Party was gone. A leadership vote of Alliance Party members was held, and in the second round of voting, Stockwell Day beat Preston Manning for leadership of the new party.

Day won the leadership in July, 2000, and in October a general election was called for November 27. The Liberals won that election with 41% of the vote and 172 seats, while the Alliance under Day received 26% of the vote and 66 seats, most of which were in the West. Ontario had voted overwhelmingly Liberal. Reform had been folded into the Alliance with the expectation that the new party would "unite the right" and oust the Liberals. This plan had failed.

AFTERMATH OF THE 2000 ELECTION

For many western conservatives, there seemed to be no hope in sight. Three federal Liberal election victories were three too many. Now was the time for the West to separate. The result of the November 2000 federal election was to incite new sympathy for separatism in parts of western Canada, especially Alberta.

Ironically, one of the first public voices advocating Alberta separatism was from Ontario. Ian Hunter, professor emeritus of law at the University of Western Ontario, wrote:

> For the West (particularly Alberta and BC) the way forward is out.If the West is finally fed up with Liberal governments foisted upon them by Ontario, it is time to go it alone.

> The creation of the Reform Party (with its slogan "The West Wants In") took the steam out of an incipient western separatist movement. It will now revive (Hunter 2000, 16).

Hunter was quite right. The movement did revive.

Western separatism was once again an important topic in the press. Former BC Liberal leader Gordon Gibson wrote favourably of BC separatism in the *National Post*, for example. *National Post* columnist Andrew Coyne wrote against it (Grace 2001a, 9).

The Report newsmagazine (successor to *Alberta Report*) was once again in the forefront of the discussion. For example, associate editor Paul Bunner wrote the following about western independence: "In the wake of the November federal election, there can be no doubt that this is the West's necessary and inevitable destiny, and almost every day brings more evidence that the East-West split in the country is unbridgeable" (Bunner 2001a, 2).

Ted Byfield wrote that Canada needed a new constitutional arrangement that would be better for the West. But the West wouldn't have any bargaining chips unless separation was a real option. As he put it, "The only way we can change Canada is to develop ways of getting out of Canada. We must posses other options" (Byfield, T., 2001a, 60). This is how it would work, in Byfield's view:

> Unless we make credible threats to set up on our own we will get absolutely nothing by way of constitutional change, or any other kind of change. We will be bashed down every time. If we threatened to leave and meant

it, we would have enormous clout in Canada, more even than Quebec. By refusing to entertain such an idea, we have no clout whatever. That is the message of history – and of the last three federal elections (Byfield, T., 2001a, 60).

Early in 2001, the AIP suddenly began to attract considerable attention. The main figure in the AIP was Cory Morgan, an oil field surveyor. He had actually begun working on building the party in 1998. It was largely the Supreme Court of Canada's *Vriend* decision that pushed him into separatist activism. The Court in that decision compelled Alberta to protect homosexual rights in its human rights legislation. Although Morgan was himself a social liberal and did not oppose homosexual rights, he did not think that federal judges should be dictating Alberta's laws. As he explains it:

> I viewed the Supreme Court ruling forcing us to "read in" aspects to our provincially modeled human rights legislation to be an unforgivable federal intrusion on provincial rights. Why should we bother building and trying to implement provincial legislation when it can essentially be re-written on our behalf by federally appointed judges? At that time it was clear that the majority of Albertans did not support that ruling thus the will of the democratically elected provincial government was overruled by justices that had no respect or concerns for the wishes of the provinces.

> I see the parliamentary system as outdated and fatally flawed. The failures of the Meech Lake and Charlottetown accords demonstrated that even modest constitutional reform is virtually impossible to achieve within Canada much less any form of significant change. I concluded that what is required in order for the nation of Canada to be rebuilt is for the confederation to be torn down first. The secession of a province would be the only catalyst that could lead to this. Even if a form of reconfederation never came about in a post Alberta secession world, the province of Alberta would still be

better off to pursue her own interests alone (Morgan 2008a).

Initially, he tried to find an existing separatist party. The closest thing around was the Doug Christie WCC. After attending one of its meetings, he concluded that a different organization was needed. He began work to form the AIP by creating a website. He was able to collect about 40 people dedicated to the new party. However, the effort to register a new party – especially gathering the necessary 6000 signatures for registration – was a difficult hurdle to leap. He and some of his supporters thus joined the Alberta Party (the old Alberta Political Alliance of 1986) to see if it could be converted into a separatist party, but that effort didn't work (Morgan 2008a).

The results of the November 2000 federal election breathed new life into the AIP. Morgan relates:

> The 2000 election was certainly a turning point. The focus of the election was strongly East/West and the rhetoric against Alberta was strong as I am sure that you recall. The fury in Alberta was clear on election day and we decided it was time to move with the Alberta Party. We had almost managed to stack the board. Valerie Clark, Barry McMillan, Stacey Barrett, Brian Twigg and myself tried to shove through a policy change for the party and failed by a small margin.

> We then left the Alberta Party along with some of their members and refocused on trying to get the AIP going. The website was built back into a partisan look again and a press release was issued. The National Post and Calgary Herald picked up on it and things began to take off for the fledgling movement (Morgan 2008a).

Most AIP members at this point had only recently become separatists, and Morgan guessed that "upwards of 80%" had been Reform Party members (Morgan 2008a).

The AIP held its founding convention in Red Deer, January 21-22, 2001. About 250 people attended, including two Canadian Alliance MPs as well as the two men who had been elected as Alberta's senatorsin-waiting, Bert Brown and Prof. Ted Morton. Prime Minister Jean Chretien and federal cabinet minister Stephane Dion both publicly expressed concern about the MPs' attendance. "Suddenly Alberta separatism was more lively than at any time since the halcyon year of 1982" (Grace 2001b, 15).

The following month, Alberta Premier Ralph Klein called a provincial general election for March. The AIP could not get registered in time for the election, so its candidates had to run as independents. It managed to recruit 15 independent candidates, but none of them even came close to winning a seat. Four of them received at least 8% of the vote in their ridings.

Shortly before the election was called, Ted Byfield wrote a column explaining the benefits of having some AIP MLAs elected (Byfield, T., 2001b, 60). Paul Bunner expressed a similar thought saying:

> If the AIP gets party status before Premier Ralph Klein drops the writ, presumably there will be a handful of candidates running on the separatist ticket in the March election. As long as they're not tangled up with some of the modern retro-Social Credit groups that obsess about international bankers' conspiracies and promote oddball monetary theories, it wouldn't hurt to park a few votes with them (Bunner 2001b, 2).

However, the party did not even register and its few candidates did not fare particularly well. Cory Morgan described the situation this way:

> While we were a dedicated group, most of us involved in forming the party were not experienced in such organization and were terribly naive. When the party hit the news after the 2000 election, we surged from 100 members to over 2000 within a few months. We were not prepared for that and were terribly organized. The lack of registration was terribly hindering us as we could not properly fundraise or advertise during an election. We still took the registration for granted however and did not put enough resources into petitioning. While a couple thousand people were willing to spend $10 to call themselves members, it was

terrifically difficult to get people to even sign a petition much less go out and petition others. Shortly before the provincial election of 2001, we sent a mail-out to over 2000 people with an enclosed form asking them to simply get friends and family to sign and to return the form. We got about 30 letters back and perhaps 200 signatures within them. We tried putting an insert into the Grande Prairie newspaper with the petition form in it (at great expense) to see how that would work. That got us about another 30 signatures.

When Klein called the election in February, we were still about 2000 signatures short. We would not be able to register mid-election anyway as the electoral office was tied up. Our next course of action was to try and field over 42 candidates in the election which would get us instant registration. We had over 80 people express that they were willing to put their names forth for that. On nomination day, it turned out that we had 15 people who actually followed through.

After the election interest in the party and separatism in general seemed to vanish overnight. We learned about the fickle nature of politics. Getting the remaining signatures in time was looking impossible. The thousands already gathered were gathered by a handful of people who were now tired and dejected (Morgan 2008a).

The party also had to deal with divisions between soft-line and hard-line separatists. It had taken an officially soft-line approach at the January convention, but struggles between those supporting both approaches continued into the fall of 2001 (Cosh 2001, 4). Then, in December, the party folded.

This was not the end of efforts to create a separatist party for Alberta, however. The attempt to take over the Alberta Party failed, but a subsequent attempt to take over the Alberta First Party succeeded. Taking control of an existing registered party saved all of the effort needed to obtain registration for a new party.

The Alberta First Party was taken over by separatists in June 2004. The party's name was then changed to the Separation Party of Alberta. Separation Party leader Bruce Hutton explained what happened as follows:

> The leader of the Alberta First party (John Riel) ran for the leadership of the Alberta Liberal party. There was no executive in place for the Alberta First Party so we bought memberships and took over the party. This was with Mr. Riel's blessing. We then called a special meeting of the membership of the as yet unregistered Separation Party of Alberta and moved to merge with the Alberta First Party. We then passed a special resolution changing the name of the Party to the Separation Party of Alberta (Hutton 2008).

The Separation Party ran 12 candidates in the November 2004 Alberta general election. None of them even came close to winning, and the proportion of votes each candidate received was quite small. Cory Morgan ran for the Separation Party in the Highwood riding, but received only about 3% of the vote there.

In the next Alberta general election, in March 2008, the Separation Party only ran one candidate, party leader Bruce Hutton. He received only a little over 1% of the vote in his riding. Hutton noted that "Interest or even talk of separation had waned with Mr. Harper in Ottawa." Nevertheless, "We ran one candidate in 2008 to keep our party registered, as this is a requirement under the Alberta Elections Act regulations" (Hutton 2008).

In the 2008 Alberta election, Cory Morgan ran as a candidate of the Wildrose Alliance Party (WAP) rather than for the Separation Party. This reflected some change in his thinking. Rather than advocating the election of a separatist party to take Alberta out of Confederation, Morgan now thinks separation should result from a referendum. "The time for Alberta to go on her own will come, though I will not hazard a guess as to exactly when. At that time, the decision will be made by Albertans in a referendum, not by a party" (Morgan 2008b).

The WAP believes in citizen initiated referenda and it respects the federal Clarity Act, which lays out the process for a province to pull out of Canada. As well, the Alberta government needs to have its own house put in order before separation makes sense. If the government in Edmonton is making a mess of things, what sense would it make for that government to receive the powers of a national government? Morgan explains his current thinking this way:

> The place of Alberta within (or out of) confederation should be determined by the citizens rather than a party. Legislation for increased direct democracy would help empower us in that regard.
>
> I think deep inside many Albertans may see the hypocrisy that we demonstrate. In that I mean that most of the changes that we have demanded furiously with the Reform Party federally have never actually been demonstrated provincially. Our legislature is no more democratic than our parliament. Our provincial spending has been no more restrained or responsible than the federal spending has. Access to information, HRCs etc are all the same within our province as they are federally.
>
> How can we really convince ourselves that we would be better off as an independent state when we have not really managed to clean up our own back yard?
>
> Federal waste and incompetence will surely fan secessionist feelings in Alberta. We will need to be confident that we are better than that in order for those feelings to truly set in though. That means we must prove through our own actions that we will indeed do better on our own. That means that provincial reform must come first. (Morgan 2008b).

Once Alberta's own government has been cleaned up, the way would be clear for the province to move towards independence, via a referendum. The WAP is the vehicle for those who accept this line of reasoning.

PROFESSOR LEON CRAIG

Alberta separatism received a shot in the arm in July 2005, when one of the province's most prestigious political scientists wrote an article for the *Calgary Herald,* advocating that Albertans should "Declare our independence - withdraw from the Canadian federation, become an independent commonwealth with our own sovereign government, directly answerable to no one but the people of Alberta" (Craig 2005, D6). Craig was a professor emeritus of political science at the University of Alberta, so intellectually, he was a force to be reckoned with.

Craig was not arguing, like Ted Byfield, that Alberta should threaten separation as a means to achieving favourable constitutional concessions from central Canada. He was arguing that Alberta should be its own country: "We should undertake a move toward independence with a whole-hearted intention of achieving it, not as simply a tactic whereby to get (temporarily) a 'better deal' from Ottawa (i.e., get some of our money back, provided as a sop to assuage 'western alienation')" (Craig 2005, D6).

His line of argument was primarily cultural, as opposed to economic. He reiterated the basic economic argument about Albertans being better off financially if the province became independent. But that was not his main point. He believed that eastern Canada's culture had deteriorated beyond recovery, and that by remaining within Canada, Alberta would decline along with the East. As Craig put it, "what makes Canada's political sickness practically incurable is that a substantial majority of the citizens east of Thunder Bay are essentially debased" (Craig 2005, D6). So Albertans need to get out: "if we remain subject to the decadent cultural and moral influence of central Canada for another generation, we will ourselves become increasingly infected with the qualities that since the Trudeau era have come to define Canadian 'national' character - sanctimonious, resentful, whining, spiteful, hypocritical, preening, cowardly, feckless, weak" (Craig 2005, D6).

He summed up his case as follows:

> As a ship of state, Canada is structurally unsound, sailing aimlessly in a perpetual fog, captained by an endless succession of faux-genteel poseurs, pilferers,

con artists and outright crooks.

Sooner or later, it is bound to end up on the rocks and founder, and there is nothing we Albertans can do about that.

But there is no reason for us to go down with it (Craig 2005, D6).

From September 29-October 1, 2006, the Citizens Centre for Freedom and Democracy held a large meeting in Calgary known as the Calgary Congress. Its purpose was to discuss ways to improve how Canada is governed, especially from a western viewpoint. As a result of his *Calgary Herald* article, Prof. Craig was invited to present a talk arguing for Alberta's independence.

During his talk, Craig added an interesting point for Albertans to consider. He asked, "If you were *already* independent, would you consider *joining* Canada under the same conditions as obtain today?" (Craig 2006, 6). And he challenged the audience, stating that their attempts at reforming Canada would come to naught unless they threatened separation:

> [I]f you are not prepared to support an Independence movement in the event that all your best efforts *fail*, your best efforts certainly *will* fail …So, in order to prove that you are serious in your push for Reform, it seems to me that you have no choice but to adopt the position of 'Reform, or Else … Independence.' And in order to prove your seriousness about *that*, you must support an agenda that would make Independence a real possibility" (Craig 2006, 7).

According to a report published in the *Globe and Mail*, at the conclusion of Craig's talk, "the applause was extended, including cheers and a standing ovation" (Gibson 2006).

Former BC Liberal leader Gordon Gibson, who wrote this report, noted what was significant compared to previous separatist expressions:

> The question period was not just civil; it was friendly and interested.

This is quite a change from the Alberta separatism of a couple of decades ago. The speech and the dialogue was quiet and reasoned, no firebrand stuff. Prof. Craig said that this was his first and last political appearance, and anyway hard-core separatism in Alberta was probably only 10 per cent. But he may have started something. Quiet and reasoned talk is especially dangerous (Gibson 2006).

Nevertheless, it does not appear that Prof. Craig's article and speech led to any sustained, new effort on the part of Alberta separatists. But it certainly gave the cause a certain credibility. No Alberta academic had made the case for Alberta separatism since Warren Blackman, in 1982.

In January 2006, the Conservative Party of Canada won enough seats in the general election to form a minority government under leader Stephen Harper. Harper had been an early Reform Party official, and had won a seat for that party in the 1993 federal election. He was seen as a credible westerner.

In October 2008, the Conservatives under Harper again won enough seats to form a minority government. Shortly afterwards, however, the Liberals, NDP and Bloc Quebecois attempted to form a parliamentary coalition to replace the Harper government. This act outraged many westerners, who had voted for Harper by a wide margin.

As a result, there appeared to be another surge of support for separatism in Alberta. Prominent Calgary conservative activist David Crutcher founded the Western Business and Taxpayers Association as a new separatist organization (O'Neill 2009, 29). The attempt at forming a Liberal/NDP/Bloc coalition government failed, however, and it was uncertain whether the surge in separatist support would last.

CONCLUSION

The rise of the Reform Party absorbed separatist sentiment in Alberta in the late 1980s. Once it was gone, however, there was no longer a political vehicle for patriotic Albertans concerned that their province was getting a raw deal from Canada.

When the Reform Party's successor organization, the Canadian Alliance, was spurned by Ontario in the 2000 federal election, separatism again appeared in Alberta. It hasn't developed very far, but it has returned. Most patriotic Albertans trust Prime Minister Stephen Harper to defend their interests as he has a proven record of standing up for Alberta. If Harper leaves, or compromises too far in an effort to win votes in Ontario and Quebec, however, separatism in Alberta could grow again.

REFERENCES

Bunner, Paul. 2001a. "Western independence looks like a job for 007." *The Report*. February 5: 2.

Bunner, Paul. 2001b. "Give us some more of that 'tough love,' Jean." *The Report*. February 19: 2.

Byfield, Link. 1997. "Reform doesn't need Ontario and might be better off without it."*Alberta Report*. April 14: 2.

Byfield, Ted. 1997. "Six key questions and some hazarded answers on the '97 election Results." *Alberta Report*. June 16: 44.

Byfield, Ted. 2001a. "The West's paradox – the only way we can change Canada is by finding ways to leave it." *The Report*. February 5: 60.

Byfield, Ted. 2001b. "The voters in three little Alberta constituencies could decide the future of the West and Canada." *The Report*. February 19: 60.

Cosh, Colby. 2001. "Planet of the AIP." *The Report*. October 22: 4.

Craig, Leon Harold. 2005. "Let's Get While The Gettin's Good." *Calgary Herald*. July 17: D6.

Craig, Leon Harold. 2006. "Remarks Prepared for *The Calgary Congress*." Edmonton: Citizens Centre for Freedom and Democracy.

Dabbs, Frank. 1997. *Preston Manning: The Roots of Reform*. Vancouver: Greystone Books.

Gibson, Gordon. 2006. "A little friendly talk about Alberta separatism." *Globe and Mail*. October 4.

Gibson, Will, and Mike Byfield. 1999. "Will Reform re-form?" *Alberta Report*. April 19: 8-11.

Grace, Kevin Michael. 2001a. "Waiting for a Levesque." *The Report*. January 1: 9.

Grace, Kevin Michael. 2001b. "Send them a message." *The Report*. February 19: 15.

Howse, John. 1989. "Upset in the West." *Maclean's*. March 27: 12-13.

Hunter, Ian. 2000. "Message to the West: leave while you still can, there's no intelligent life down here." *The Report*. December 18: 16.

Hutton, Bruce. 2008. Personal email to the author. December 28.

Manning, Preston. 1992. *The New Canada*. Toronto: Macmillan Canada.

Morgan, Cory. 2008a. Personal email to the author. December 28.

Morgan, Cory. 2008b. Personal email to the author. December 30.

O'Neill, Terry. 2009. "Face to face." *Report Magazine*. February: 29-35.

CHAPTER 7

STEPHEN HARPER AND THE FUTURE OF ALBERTA SEPARATISM

For most of his political career, Stephen Harper has distinguished himself as a genuine Albertan, concerned with the province's well-being. There is considerable evidence of his western sympathies, notably his work on behalf of the Reform Party of Canada. In fact, for some people in other parts of Canada, Harper's identification with Alberta was seen as a black mark against him.

As prime minister, there are severe limitations on what Harper can achieve on behalf of Alberta. In terms of institutional change, he has basically nothing to show. But there is little doubt that that reflects his circumstances rather than his sympathies.

Nevertheless, if Harper fails to achieve much for Alberta while pursuing support in Ontario and Quebec, many Albertans will be disappointed. It would show, once again, that a mainstream political party is only interested in maintaining power, not helping Alberta. This can only add fuel to the separatist case.

STEPHEN HARPER AT THE
REFORM PARTY'S FOUNDING CONVENTION

At the Reform Party of Canada's founding convention, early in November 1987, Stephen Harper delivered a speech. At that time he was identified as a part-time economics lecturer at the University of Calgary. Many people considered his speech to be a highlight of the convention. Two large excerpts of the speech were subsequently published in *Alberta Report*. They reveal a strong commitment to the western position, namely, that the West was being shortchanged by Ottawa and that that had to stop.

Harper pointed out that there was a double-standard at work in Canada. The interests of central Canada were seen as Canadian interests, whereas the interests of the West were something else altogether. Canada had developed:

> a highly centralized political culture which is inherently and righteously biased against western Canada in its basic values and rhetoric. Whenever challenged, it wraps itself in a flag called "Canadian identity," "Canadian nationalism," "national unity," or the "national interest."

> For example, protection of the American-owned automobile industry in Oshawa under the Auto Pact is in the "national interest." But the American-owned energy industry in Calgary should be subject to "Canadianization." Foreign investment is labeled "American economic colonialism" when, to westerners, it is rather a source of funds outside the centralized and concentrated Canadian banking system. The whole concept of "Canadian culture" no longer means the values and lifestyles of Canadians in a diverse country.

Instead it means the protection of narrow arts and media interest groups based in Toronto. Unilingualism in Quebec is a legitimate desire – *maitres chez nous*. In Manitoba, it is "redneck" and "racist" (Harper 1987a, 17).

Harper talked a lot about the usual western complaints concerning a lack of economic fairness in Canada. The West was not receiving its appropriate share of federal expenditures, for instance. And there was the substantial amount of money Ottawa had hauled out of Alberta due to oil pricing and fiscal transfers. The Alberta recession of the mid-1980s helped to underscore the federal government's hypocrisy:

> The recent downturns in the western economy have provoked lectures on how we are dependent on international prices. Of course, this defence was not appropriate when there was a boom here. Then westerners were told that central Canada could not pay the prices set in international markets (Harper 1987a, 15).

Despite this problem, however, Harper adamantly rejected separatism. His view was that the West deserved much better treatment because it had been a positive contributor to Canada:

> To achieve economic justice, we maintain that the West need not demonstrate a desire to leave Confederation to get better treatment. Rather, the West must receive better treatment because it is already a member, and has been a good one. The West must receive a "Fair Shake."
>
> A Fair Shake requires the immediate dismantling and restructuring of all policies and discretionary decisions that discriminate against the West. Economic justice begins with an equality of concern that must be matched by equality of action resulting in equality of treatment (Harper 1987b, 16).

After discussing specific ways of addressing the West's concerns, Harper talked about solving the "crisis of the Welfare State." This involved shrinking the size of government, protecting property rights and privatizing crown corporations:

> Property rights should be entrenched in the Canadian constitution. As well, a more serious privatization policy should be adopted. At the top of the list should be Petro-Canada. Both federal ownership and control of Petro-Canada must be terminated so that it can never again be used as vehicle for central Canadian colonialism and expropriation. This is the critical missing link in the job of dismantling the National Energy Program (Harper 1987b, 17).

Towards the end of his speech, Harper had strong words about the need for change in Canadian politics, and in particular, the need for the Reform Party of Canada:

> In the stale air of politics, what Canada really requires is the sweeping winds of change. This will challenge the vested interests of the National Policy, the Welfare State, and the Quebec question, and they will resist. In the end, however, these groups will have to cast aside their narrow definitions of Canada – the country they claim to love – because that country can no longer be built on the economic exploitation and political disenfranchisement of western Canada.In the meantime, we require a political party to put pursuit of the West's agenda at the top of its list. This must be a party willing to end central control and special interest politics in its own ranks (Harper 1987b, 17).

Stephen Harper was a major political and economic theorist for the Reform Party of Canada in its early years. He was clearly convinced that the West required a better deal in Confederation. This was the initial overriding concern of the party, its central reason for existence. It would be the main vehicle for the political expression of pro-Alberta sentiment, from 1988 until its demise eleven years later.

Preston Manning wrote that Harper's speech was the "best speech and most influential presentation at the Founding Assembly of the Reform

Party of Canada." He added that "Harper's address to the Winnipeg Assembly was more germane to western concerns and more detailed in its analysis and its policy prescriptions than any speech by any cabinet minister to a western audience since the Conservatives came to power [in 1984]" (Manning 1992, 149).

HARPER'S SUBSEQUENT CAREER

Shortly thereafter, Harper became the Reform Party's first policy chief. When Deborah Grey was elected in March 1989, Harper became her first legislative assistant while remaining the party's top policy officer. He was a key figure in the early years of the Reform Party and was elected as a Reform MP from Calgary in the 1993 federal election.

In early 1997, Harper resigned as an MP to work for the National Citizens Coalition, a conservative lobby group. But he continued to support a pro-western position, and he wanted the Reform Party to remain that way as well. He said, "I think it is really important that Reform see itself as a western party. It's clear that the West gets more attention and has more potential clout when it has its own political vehicle" (Jenkinson 1997, 10).

Harper's continued pro-Alberta perspective was clearly on display shortly after the November 2000 federal election. He was one of the six prominent citizens who wrote an open letter to Premier Ralph Klein, suggesting that Alberta "build firewalls" around itself to limit federal interference. Known as the "firewall letter," its proposals became known as the "Alberta Agenda."

The policy ideas suggested in the letter were for Alberta to have its own pension plan instead of the Canada Pension Plan, to collect its own personal income tax, to create its own provincial police force in place of the RCMP, to exercise greater control of its health care policy and to attempt to force senate reform back onto the national agenda. All of these proposals were within the existing constitutional jurisdiction of the provinces, so they were not revolutionary, by any means. Nevertheless, the letter did set out a very Alberta-centric policy initiative.

Harper and his associates believed their firewall agenda was necessary, in light of the 2000 federal election. As they saw it, during the election campaign "the Chretien government undertook a series of attacks not merely designed to defeat its partisan opponents, but to marginalize Alberta and Albertans within Canada's political system" (Harper et al 2001). They also suggested that should the country fall into a recession:

> the government in Ottawa will be tempted to take advantage of Alberta's prosperity, to redistribute income from Alberta to residents of other provinces in order to keep itself in power. It is imperative to take the initiative, to build firewalls around Alberta, to limit the extent to which an aggressive and hostile federal government can encroach upon legitimate provincial jurisdiction (Harper et al 2001).

As *The Report* magazine put it, this letter was "nothing less than the opening salvo in a campaign to make Albertans 'masters in their own house'" (Grace 2001, 10).

Stephen Harper had a consistent track record of defending the West. Whether as a Reform Party official and MP, or as a co-author of the firewall letter, his position was unmistakably pro-Alberta. When he declared his candidacy for the leadership of the Canadian Alliance at the end of 2001, his provincial rights perspective was seen by some as a red flag. He was denounced as "a provincial extremist" who was not suited to lead a national party. Confronted with this accusation, he replied in an interview:

> Look, my record is clear – I'm not a centralist. I'm a believer in division of powers between the federal and provincial governments and in provincial autonomy in resources and other matters. But I'm an opponent of separation and certainly of unilateral separation (Grace 2002, 10).

Of course, Harper went on to win the leadership of the Canadian Alliance in 2002. By the end of 2003, he had successfully worked for the merger of the Alliance and federal PC Party into the new Conservative Party of Canada. In January 2006, his party won enough parliamentary seats to form a minority government. A subsequent federal election in October 2008 gave the Conservatives more seats, but not enough to form a majority government. It was this situation that tempted the Liberals and NDP into a proposed coalition with the Bloc Quebecois in an attempt to oust Harper's minority government.

Harper has been prime minister continuously since early 2006. The kinds of institutional changes demanded by the Reform Party to benefit the West (especially senate reform) have not been implemented. But Harper still enjoys rock solid support in Alberta. Albertans are "safe" with Harper in Ottawa. His government is not likely to come after Alberta's resources in an effort to win support in other parts of the country.

Nevertheless, not all Albertans will have limitless patience with Harper. Despite his bona fides as an Alberta rights supporter, he will likely have to make choices at some point that won't go over well in the province.

Separatist-minded Albertans are already becoming skeptical. When I asked Cory Morgan if he thought Harper was doing a good job in protecting Alberta's interests in Ottawa, he replied:

> Harper is protecting Alberta better than the other federal alternatives would. That really is not saying much, however.
>
> Harper has two choices. He can protect the interests of Alberta and take a certain path back to the opposition benches, or he can cater to central Canada in hopes of gaining a majority. I suspect a majority (and maintaining it) is what will always be in Harper's eye (Morgan 2008a).

When Bruce Hutton, leader of the Separation Party of Alberta, was asked the same question, he too expressed concern:

> Mr. Harper is not in a position to protect Alberta's interests. He is the leader of a minority government – actually a government that may be replaced by a coalition. Although Harper is one of the authors of the Alberta Agenda, he would never as leader, support or in any way be responsible for any of the component

parts of that undertaking. Although it is sad to say this, "Absolute power corrupts absolutely". Unfortunately I do not personally believe Mr. Harper would help Alberta (equal senate representation or some other modified form of government to protect regions) even if he had a majority government. No one and I do mean no one wants to open up the Constitution of Canada for revision (Hutton 2008).

Harper is doing better than anyone else could do, but he's hampered by Canada's political realities. He cannot offend the large block of voters in Ontario and Quebec that keep him in power.

Despite those limitations, Albertans will probably never again have a prime minister as sympathetic to their concerns as Stephen Harper. Once he is gone, the prospects for Alberta separatism could increase substantially.

CONCLUSION

Stephen Harper has a long track record of defending Alberta's interests, so his sympathies are not in doubt. But his own interests currently entail appealing for support in Ontario and Quebec in order to maintain or enlarge his parliamentary caucus. Canadian reality forces him down a heavily-trod path – one that has exasperated many Albertans in the past. Every federal government has the incentive to cater to Ontario and Quebec while neglecting Alberta. This is a standard argument for Alberta separatism.

When Stephen Harper leaves office, however, the situation could get even worse. The next prime minister will probably not be from Alberta, and he or she will have even less reason to defend the province's interests. Thus, in my view, Alberta separatism has a future.

REFERENCES

Grace, Kevin Michael. 2001. "Alberta first." *The Report*. February 19: 10-14.

Grace, Kevin Michael. 2002. "Stephen Harper: *The Report* Interview." *The Report*. January 7: 10-11.

Harper, Stephen. 1987a. "A question of fairness." *Alberta Report*. November 16: 15, 17.

Harper, Stephen. 1987b. "Blueprint for a New National Policy." *Alberta Report*. November 23: 16-17.

Harper, Stephen, Tom Flanagan, Ted Morton, Rainer Knopff, Andrew Crooks and Ken Boessenkool. 2001. "An open letter to Ralph Klein." *National Post*. January 24.

Hutton, Bruce. 2008. Personal email to the author. December 28.

Jenkinson, Michael. 1997. "Fight each other or win separately." *Alberta Report*. April 21: 6-10.

Manning, Preston. 1992. *The New Canada*. Toronto: Macmillan Canada.

Morgan, Cory. 2008a. Personal email to the author. December 28.

CHAPTER 8

CONCLUSION

THE ALBERTA SEPARATIST MOVEMENT HAS A PAST AND IT HAS a future. Indeed, one purpose of this book is to argue that the Alberta separatist movement may very well have a period of growth in the next few years. The potential is there.

Something happened in 1980 that forever changed the way Albertans feel about Canada. Before 1980, the Alberta separatist movement had virtually no support. Even during the energy war of the 1970s, concerned Albertans put their trust in Premier Peter Lougheed and the provincial and federal Progressive Conservative parties. It wasn't long, however, before the federal PC Party demonstrated that this trust was misplaced.

In the mid-1970s, the Independent Alberta Association (IAA) was able to make occasional headlines, largely because its leadership consisted of prominent citizens. It also commissioned significant academic research. But despite these two strengths, the organization disappeared within four or five years. The idea of Alberta becoming independent did not resonate with the province, even as a scare tactic to demand more from the federal government. In the late 1970s, the Alberta separatist movement wasn't even a blip on the radar screen.

The 1980 federal election and the subsequent NEP did more than provoke a separatist surge in Alberta. It gave the idea of Alberta separatism a form of credibility it had not had before. Not credibility in the sense that people saw Alberta's independence as a real possibility, but credibility in the sense that someone could suggest it without automatically being considered a wing-nut. Among some Albertans, to declare support for separatism is now considered to be a run-of-the-mill, almost automatic reaction to stupidity in Ottawa.

Since the Alberta separatist phenomenon of the early 1980s, separatism has reappeared in public discussion a number of times in Alberta. For example, a potential resurgence of separatism was in the headlines in 1986, especially after the Mulroney government's CF-18 decision. Other examples would be the outburst after the 2000 federal election, and in December 2008, when the opposition parties in Ottawa tried to overthrow the Harper Conservative government. It's not unusual anymore for Alberta separatism to appear whenever Alberta faces some sort of showdown with the Ottawa government. This was not the case before 1980.

Thanks to Pierre Trudeau and his government, Alberta politics will never be the same. There will always be Albertans who are willing to jump in the lifeboat of independence when the federal government looms in a threatening manner. This is a new feature of Alberta life, historically speaking. In this respect, we may say that Pierre Trudeau is the father of Alberta separatism.

Could the Alberta separatist movement ever be successful? That depends on how you measure success. The odds of Alberta actually leaving Confederation are remote, at this point.

But there is a better standard by which to measure the movement's success. By the very fact of its existence, the movement constrains the ability of the federal government to enact policies that are harmful to Alberta. The existence of the separatist movement acts as a deterrent to Trudeau-style policies emanating from Ottawa.

Look at Quebec. When various federal policies are being considered, the expected reaction from Quebec nationalists is factored into the political calculation. Everyone knows what happens if the feds enflame them, and no one wants to go down that road, yet again. Thus, certain options are ruled out. If Alberta was to maintain a credible separatist movement, it's not inconceivable that the same kind of calculation would be made concerning the reaction of patriotic Albertans. But if Albertans are simply expected to roll over with any federal intrusion, the political calculation would be much different. In this respect a separatist movement is beneficial to Alberta's interests.

By this way of thinking, the best situation even for a federalist would be the existence of a credible Alberta separatist movement within a united Canada. That sounds paradoxical and ironic. How could a separatist movement benefit the country? By deterring grossly anti-Alberta policies, that's how.

Federal politicians would be less likely to enact anti-Alberta policies if a credible separatist movement were ready to whip up public anger in response. Thus, such policies probably wouldn't be proposed and tension between Alberta and the federal government would remain at a low level, enhancing national unity.

But the separatist movement needs to be more than just a negative reaction to what occurs in Ottawa. Any meaningful political movement is more than opposition to something. Richard Cleroux saw this point well in 1981, stating, "To move ahead, western separatism must start thinking in terms of nation-building. A nation cannot be built on negativism. Alberta separatists must create a new western Canadian identity to replace their existing Canadian identity" (Cleroux 1981, 117).

Another problem that has continually plagued Alberta separatism is the leadership deficit. Time and again, observers have noted that the movement lacked high calibre leadership. There were high calibre members in separatist organizations at times, but the leadership didn't measure up.

The best explanation for this phenomenon is probably the one offered by Mike Byfield, who served as the Calgary communications director for West-Fed during 1981. He explains the situation this way:

> I think I know the answer to the poor-leadership, good-membership puzzle. When a population becomes alarmed, the first people to act are often individuals with hair-trigger temperaments. This speedy response may be due to a variety of reasons, good and bad. A personality may be exceptionally virtuous or intelligent. Alternatively, the would-be leader may be merely dissatisfied with life in general or eager for power which he could not acquire through conventional organizations due to flaws in his personal character. Whatever their motives, these individuals form organizations. As popular reaction swells, more members naturally flow into these already-established political channels, just as we Calgarians gravitated toward West-Fed (Byfield 2003, 41).

Alberta separatism will likely need to solve the leadership puzzle before it breaks out of the margins.

Besides what has already been mentioned, there are two other major problems that separatists need to consider: 1) Separatists have never even agreed among themselves about the form of government and constitution that an independent Alberta would have; and, 2) The conventional oil that is the foundation for Alberta's wealth is running out.

Setting up a new government is no easy task. And it's more difficult if the people involved don't agree on what form that government should take. The differences among separatists have been substantial. Should an independent Alberta retain the monarchy or become a republic? Should it remain on its own or attempt to have the other western provinces join it? If other provinces join, what form of government will be used for the new federation? Becoming independent only to fight over the form of government would be silly. Adopting a defective form of government would certainly be worse than leaving Canada.

Right from the time the IAA released its first significant economic analysis of 1974, the economic case for Alberta's independence has been based on the province's oil wealth. However, that oil wealth has been drained continuously for the 35 years since that report was issued. Alberta is closer now to running out of conventional oil than at any previous time. The longer the time-span between now and Alberta's independence, the less oil wealth there will be to support the province's economy. Imagine Alberta becoming independent only to find that the wealth was gone. It would make more sense to stay in Canada.

In short, there are still significant intellectual hurdles over which Albertans must leap in order to make a compelling case for independence.

By the late 1970s, there was a perception among some people in Canada that power was shifting to the West, especially Alberta. This view was largely based on economics, i.e., Alberta's new oil wealth. But Ted Byfield pointed out that no real power shift had actually occurred. Economically, Alberta was growing fast, for sure, but real power would also require intellectual and cultural influence, and this had not occurred.

He went on to argue that English Canada had lost its sense of purpose. Ontario, the Maritimes, and even the West had forgotten why they existed, and this situation created a national vacuum. That vacuum created an opportunity for Alberta to truly become a centre of power:

> If out of the new western Canada that the past decade has manifested in Alberta there can come a way of life, a set of values, a philosophy that fills this national vacuum, then power will indeed shift westward. But prosperity alone won't do it. Particularly, a prosperity that is based principally on taller and more numerous branch offices.

> The precise shape of such a philosophy may be obscure but its direction becomes clearer every day. We need with all haste to revert to fundamentals. We need to teach right and wrong to our children. We need to restore structure to education. We need to instill respect for work well done. We need to preach responsibilities rather than right, sacrifice rather than gratification,

self-denial rather than self-fulfillment. All this is very far from that which we are now in fact doing. But what we are doing doesn't work. If Alberta discovers it first and corrects the situation, then power will follow from this as surely as spring follows winter or dawn from the night (Byfield 1979, 44).

Perhaps that's too much to ask for, too idealistic. But it doesn't hurt to dream, and it's a positive vision that could benefit the whole country.

Some may argue that an Alberta-based conservative philosophy has already influenced the entire Canadian polity through the Reform Party, the deficit-fighting example of Ralph Klein's government, and the "Calgary School" of political thought. There may be some truth to that. But what Byfield is pointing towards entails more than shrinking the size of government, although that would certainly be a component of it. He's talking about much more: the revitalization of the traditional morality and virtues of Western civilization.

If Alberta could recapture the philosophy that made the Western world great, it would become the intellectual or cultural centre of a revitalized country. The sense of powerlessness that often fuels the desire for an independent Alberta would be gone. And Albertans could be justifiably proud of their achievement.

REFERENCES

Byfield, Mike. 2003. "West-Fed: political lessons from a failed movement." *Citizens Centre Report*. June: 39-41.

Byfield, Ted. 1979. "The big shift of power westward: A great thing except it didn't Happen." *Alberta Report*. December 28: 44.

Cleroux, Richard. 1981. "Separatism in Quebec & Alberta." In *Western Separatism: The Myths, Realities and Dangers*, eds. Larry Pratt and Garth Stevenson. Edmonton: Hurtig Publishers Ltd.

CPSIA information can be obtained
at www.ICGtesting.com
Printed in the USA
LVHW112240031119
636132LV00005B/1/P

9 781927 684320